MW00911874

Hope Deferred

FINDING JOY BEFORE
THE HARVEST

To Pat,
Job 23:10 He knows!
Carole Dougherty

Carole Dougherty

WESTBOW
P R E S S®
A DIVISION OF THOMAS NELSON
& ZONDERVAN

Copyright © 2017 Carole Dougherty.

All rights reserved. No part of this book may be used or reproduced by any means, graphic, electronic, or mechanical, including photocopying, recording, taping or by any information storage retrieval system without the written permission of the author except in the case of brief quotations embodied in critical articles and reviews.

This book is a work of non-fiction. Unless otherwise noted, the author and the publisher make no explicit guarantees as to the accuracy of the information contained in this book and in some cases, names of people and places have been altered to protect their privacy.

Author Credits:
Ann VosKamp, Francis Chan, Oswald Chambers, E. M. Bounds, Corey Tenboom, Brother Lawrence, Richard Foster, Andrew Murray,

WestBow Press books may be ordered through booksellers or by contacting:

WestBow Press
A Division of Thomas Nelson & Zondervan
1663 Liberty Drive
Bloomington, IN 47403
www.westbowpress.com
1 (866) 928-1240

Because of the dynamic nature of the Internet, any web addresses or links contained in this book may have changed since publication and may no longer be valid. The views expressed in this work are solely those of the author and do not necessarily reflect the views of the publisher, and the publisher hereby disclaims any responsibility for them.

ISBN: 978-1-5127-9710-7 (sc)
ISBN: 978-1-5127-9711-4 (hc)
ISBN: 978-1-5127-9709-1 (e)

Library of Congress Control Number: 2017911882

Print information available on the last page.

WestBow Press rev. date: 08/28/2017

A special thanks to the gals on my prayer team.
You know who you are.
You have pushed, pulled, carried, and dragged me for years,
and I love you for it.

… And to my husband and children,
who still
take my breath away.

Contents

Acknowledgments

To my dear friend and in-law Amie Sauvan, Addison's mom. Since I had never written a book, her experience and background in marketing became essential as she helped me find a platform I didn't even know existed. As my publicist, she has helped me edit, served as my personal thesaurus, and helped me navigate through the technical *stuff*. She has been a silent partner through this journey, aching in the wings and lending counsel and support when she needed to be receiving it herself. Our lunch dates were life support for me, and I eagerly anticipated them. She is the cheerleader everyone hopes to have in their corner. Thank you, Amie. I love you.

To Kelly Reynolds, whom I highly treasure as a literary assistant. She believed strongly in me telling this story, and with her good eye and sharp mind, she kept me on track to make it happen. With motivational and editorial help, she pushed me forward critiquing and revising with love and support. Kelly has a feel for the rhythm of a book, and I found her insight crucial and refreshing. She gave me the confidence to go to print and made the journey just plain *fun*.

Introduction

We are always waiting for something. As a child, except for one day a year, I was waiting for Christmas. In junior high it was my first boyfriend, and in high school it was the results of cheerleading tryouts.

But waiting for your *fun meter* to go to the top is much different than waiting—sometimes for years—for a crisis to be averted or pain and suffering to end. How are we, as believers, supposed to give thanks and find joy while we wait?

"Hope deferred makes the heart sick, but a longing fulfilled is a tree of life" (Proverbs 13:12 NIV). How do we live with the waiting? Can we thrive and not just survive this delay?

Oh, the wisdom of God to not let us see our future. I have lived most of my life fearing it rather than anticipating it. Not anymore.

In the midst of a debilitating and mysterious illness that plagued our family for more than a decade, I found the joy that had eluded me for years. I found happiness and even contentment before my prayers were answered. I discovered peace before my *harvest* arrived.

You may be waiting for God to bring you that perfect spouse, a prodigal child to return home, or your bosses at work to finally recognize you and offer you that promotion. Can we find joy when God is refusing to give us that one thing we feel we need to be happy? *Why does he refuse? Is it something I've done wrong? Am I being punished? Am I not doing enough?*

God is the Lord of the harvest, and only he knows when the harvest is ready. I have learned that the garden is still a beautiful place to be while I am watching his handiwork unfold. And through the entire growth season, he never let go of our hands.

My desire in writing this book is for you to know how much God loves you and wants to walk with you while your hope is being deferred. Let him give you unspeakable joy in the wait.

Chapter 1

Breaking Fallow Ground

I imagine it is because I grew up in a small Kansas town, the oldest of six, that I envisioned my enchanted future as one living rurally with lots of children. In my daydream, I pictured myself on the porch steps of a stately and old white farmhouse, baby in tow, with little ones peeking out from behind me. It was probably my neighbor taking the photo because my husband would be out on a combine, working the lower forty. This spoke happiness and peace to me.

My mom stayed home with us when we were young. It was very reassuring that she took the job of preparing us for life very seriously ... and loved doing it. She was a strong-willed, intelligent woman who could succeed on many paths, but she felt this was the most important one to throw her passions into. She came to know Jesus at twenty-one, already a mother to four, and hit the road running with energy and a new zest for life.

Then there was my dad. He did not know the joy or peace that comes with knowing Christ, so he viewed this life through a very different lens. Without looking at life through God's Word, there are no filters. Death, life, pain, sorrow, accidents—all are random. Even successes and triumphs end up seeming empty of purpose.

The loss of innocence—we all go through it. I know with my own children I had hoped it would be an easy transition. It could be working the customer service at a big-box store and seeing that all people were not kind or honest. Or it could be experiencing angry drivers honking at them as they sweated behind a steering wheel, trying to earn their restricted driver's license. Then as their realistic experiences increased, hopefully, their walk with Christ would too, and it would all balance out. Ha! That has been the exception, not the rule.

The September after I turned fourteen, my thirteen-year-old sister Nancy was hit by a car as she was walking to school. I was retrieved from gym class to go home and stay with our younger siblings as I learned my mom was in an ambulance heading to Kansas City. My sister was given no chance to live, and for the first two weeks, I was given all of her gifts that well-wishers brought as they visited and encouraged my parents. I still can't smell Avon's Moonwind to this day without it feeling dark and haunting.

Weeks went by, and Nancy would survive her coma. But the brain damage was severe, and she would need to learn everything over again—from counting to reciting her ABC's. With my sister in a body cast until Christmas, my mom practically lived at the hospital, which was an hour away. Nancy would miss most of her eighth-grade year, and I had to help the family by running the home while Mom was away. My loss of innocence had officially begun.

I have no memories of my dad being around during that time. He lived there, but his relationship with all of us slowly faded until he was just gone three years later. I took way more emotional responsibility on my shoulders than I should have. My mom felt it too, so one summer she encouraged me to accept a job at a Christian camp in Colorado.

For two months before I left, I suffered from insomnia. When my siblings rose in the morning, I usually hadn't slept at all. The house was quiet, and the nights were long when I was up alone. It just felt so irresponsible leaving my mom by herself with our family. That was the saddest season in my life—at least so far.

───────※※───────

Three years after Nancy's accident in the fall of my senior year, my father walked out of our lives. He left behind an overwhelmed wife, five broken daughters, and one bewildered son, who would now try to transition into manhood alone. When Dad left, he stayed gone. But my mom helped us learn to make peace with all of it.

When he left, my mom determined she was not going to have a bunch of dysfunctional adults on her hands. She taught us how to turn our anger and self-pity into feelings of sorrow for our dad. From that time on, anytime someone genuinely wronged us, Mom had us visualize looking down on them in a pit. We did not put them there. It was not our fault that they were there. They were missing out on so many blessings because of their poor decisions.

Could God lift them out of that pit? Absolutely! If they bent their knees and surrendered their lives to the Creator, they could be forgiven, and then God would begin the road to repair. But just like us, they were given free will, and as long as they chose to blindly stay in that hole, rejecting God's voice, they would suffer alone with their choices and regrets. We were to pray for our *enemy* and replace anger with pity. It saved our lives.

My dad's leaving meant my mom had to find work, so we left our bungalow on the corner of Castle and Kaskaskia and said goodbye to brick streets and small-town gossip and headed to Kansas City. With that move, I also left behind any security I had known, not realizing it would be years before I would find it again.

The only neighborhood we could afford was in the inner city, where police sirens lulled you to sleep at night. By this time, there were eight children in the home as my mom had taken in two lost teenagers years before. Almost overnight we went from a middle-class, blue-collar, working family to living at the poverty level. We stood in lines at school for free breakfasts and lunches. We learned of food stamps and free health clinics, and I began applying for full grants to get into college. I hated it. I was embarrassed and angry.

I had trusted Jesus at five years old right after my mom came to know him. I knew he loved me, and I have never doubted that I was his sheep. But where was he in all of this? Does he really mean it when he says, "Do not be anxious about anything" (Philippians 4:6a NIV)? Or how about in Matthew where he tells the disciples to take no thought what they should eat, drink, or even wear? I was mad at my mom for what seemed like her simple faith. Her lack of worry or concern seemed like she wasn't being responsible and didn't care. But I couldn't deny time after time God's faithfulness sliding in there at the last second. Someone would find a five-dollar bill right when we needed some gas. A neighbor would bring extra produce over from their garden when our cupboards were bare. Babysitting opportunities would arise right before a bill was due, or a little money would come in the mail from an anonymous donor. Have I mentioned that I hated living like this?

I had taken a job at Macy's in a local mall. Everyone was doing what they could to help keep us afloat. The church we had begun attending, had hired a young pastor with a wife and three children and my mom really wanted to help them get started. Although there was no extra money, she told the Lord that the next month she wanted to contribute anything that came in on a Wednesday, food or money, to this family.

Mom hadn't anticipated that the next month was November. Sure enough, the Wednesday before Thanksgiving, she realized we had nothing for the holiday meal. She also knew that if something came to us on that day, she would give it away. That evening she reassured my youngest brother and sister that God would provide a turkey dinner, and then she sent them off to bed, hopeful for tomorrow's celebration. She later told me she went in and cried herself to sleep.

An hour later she woke up and headed to the kitchen, turning on the light to get a drink. The doorbell rang, and she glanced at the clock. It was one minute after midnight on Thursday. She peeked out the door and saw a good friend and her husband, whom she had led to Christ a few years earlier.

As she opened the door, they began bringing in box after box of food for a Thanksgiving meal, apologizing for the delay and listing all of the obstacles that had prevented them from coming earlier. They said, "We finally just decided to swing by, and if your light was on, we would stop. If it wasn't, we were just going to head back out of town." That midnight miracle carried my mom for years, and though I didn't realize it then, I was slowly increasing my own faith, diminishing my fears, teaching me to trust, and breaking fallow ground.

I got married at nineteen to a young man I met the summer I went to Colorado. I vowed to never eat Ramen noodles again! We chose to live in Kansas City, and through a couple of small scholarships and a government grant, I was able to attend a local Bible college where I studied education. My twenties would have me teaching physical education in junior high and high school, coaching girls' sports, and serving as athletic director. Being in an unequally yoked marriage, he did not know Christ, eventually took its toll and the marriage ended several years later.

Divorce is a failure. There's no way around it. Nobody sets out to have their marriage dissolve that way, especially when you have already seen the destruction so up close and personal. How do people go through tough times without the Lord?

The experiences that break you down, chip away at your confidence, and sap your strength just don't seem to be controlled by a loving God at the time. I believed that I had gotten myself into this mess, so I had to use the brain God had given me to somehow pull myself out. I hoped that somehow *all things might work together for good.* Was I aware of his presence? Most of the time. Was I aware of his purpose? Rarely. Back then I didn't have the faith that Paul wrote about in Hebrews. "He persevered because he saw him who is invisible" (Hebrews 11:27b NIV). Trusting is not knowing his purpose but believing that he loves me and is doing what's best for me. It's knowing that someday our mess will open doors for his message.

In those early years, I just felt I was constantly waiting to be delivered from something. I didn't realize the process was more valuable to God than the answered prayer to "make it stop." I saw little value in the waiting and definitely found very little joy while enduring.

I find it so ironic that my name, Carole, means "song of joy" when it has eluded me most of my life. For so long I had such sadness that a sigh was much more common than a smile. I love Genesis 48:15, where Jacob, who is about to die, says that God has been his shepherd all of his life. That surety back then and the hope that God knew my struggles gave me the strength to press forward, even if it was one sigh at a time.

⁂

Of course, her middle name will be Grace. It's a given. Grace had covered my life the past few years, allowing me to find Gary, a wonderful, gentle husband, and finally, giving me the blessing to conceive a baby. Her name will be Rebekah Grace, and so it was.

At this time Big Blaine, an older brother, was seven years old. He was our eleventh attempt at adopting a child, and once again, grace ushered in this brown-eyed teddy bear. Emily Jo came next, but not until after a judge sadly ordered us to give back a little boy named Daniel, whom we had adopted more than a year before her. His biological mom simply changed her mind and wanted him back. Her lawyer found a technicality that ours had overlooked.

After the ruling, as we sat there in shock, her lawyer came to our table and asserted, "We've got a plane to catch. Hand us over the child, and we will mail you the expenses that the judge ordered my client to reimburse you for." In a whirlwind Daniel was gone, and the money never came.

Our lawyer kept encouraging us to fight, to take it to the Kansas Supreme Court. Of course, it meant more money and more time and more anger to keep it going. I thought I had made peace with it, trusting God's sovereignty. Instead, every time we received another form, another bill in the mail, I felt anxiety and depression welling up. I was done! I hated the ugliness of the fight. Children are a gift from the Lord, and he will pay for his gifts. We dropped the case cold turkey, and our peace returned.

The following year, as the anniversary of losing Daniel was near, I found myself reliving all the old feelings of hurt and

7

frustration. I found myself fighting back anger over not being able to replenish our savings for another adoption possibility. Blaine was now three, and he and I prayed every night that Jesus would help bring us a baby girl. That morning I asked the Lord again if it was his will to give our family another child. Then I dried my eyes, stuck on some praise and worship music, and finished the dishes.

At two o'clock that same afternoon, I received a phone call from a social worker saying she had a baby girl for us. I made her repeat it three times! We were to go to court on Friday to pick Emily Jo up. Friday was one year to the day that we had lost Daniel. God is amazing! His healing is complete, and his timing is perfect.

I love the passage where Jehoshaphat is facing the biggest enemy of his life. The Bible says he inquired of the Lord. He cried out, "We do not know what to do, but our eyes are upon you" (2 Chronicles 20:12c NIV). God's messenger replied, "Listen, King Jehoshaphat and all who live in Judah and Jerusalem! This is what the LORD says to you: 'Do not be afraid or discouraged because of this vast army. For the battle is not yours, but God's'" (2 Chronicles 20:15b NIV). He then told the king how to proceed, and he boldly went out against his enemies.

> After consulting the people, Jehoshaphat appointed men to sing to the Lord and to praise him for the splendor of his holiness as they went out at the head of the army, saying: "Give thanks to the LORD, for his love endures forever." As they began to sing and praise, the LORD set ambushes against the men of Ammon and Moab and Mount Seir who were invading Judah, and they were defeated. (2 Chronicles 20:21–22 NIV)

Wow! Sounds simple. Inquire of the Lord, keep our eyes on him, and start praising. We need to leave defeating the enemy to him. He's good at it.

To this day, I can't tell you where all the money came from to pay Emily's adoption bills. It's just a blur. Here and there, little by little, and it was done. We chose to trust God rather than lose our relationship with him, and he was faithful.

A couple of years went by, and I was out grocery shopping one morning. A little boy came up, jumped on the side of my cart, and just stared at me. I heard a soft voice say, "Please get away from her." I looked up to see the sister of Daniel's mom, who had been our contact person during the adoption.

I started shaking. I had often wondered how a chance encounter with his mom would end. I usually envisioned slowly walking up to her … and then decking her before slowly walking away. In reality, I left a half-filled cart of groceries in the aisle, ran out of the store to the car, and really cried for the first time over all of it. It was healing. I was done, and I knew the Lord had done it.

Two years after Rebekah was born, I gave birth to the sweetest little boy with sky-blue eyes. I recalled the verse in Isaiah that gave me strength and hope after my first marriage ended. "A bruised reed He will not break" (Isaiah 42:3a NIV). I had felt pretty beat up. And so … this child was named Reed Garrison, garrison meaning a fortress but also "Gary's son," the name of his wonderful father.

Gary had two older sons, Bobby and Billy, from an earlier marriage. Both were adopted as well and living nearby. Our cup now runneth over.

Back in a small town just outside KC, I had my rural home

with acres for hiking and planting. There was a pond just beyond my kitchen window, where I could watch the children swim and fish. I had come full circle. I was home again. But I soon realized that God did not want our roots and our domain to be our security, and he would continue to test my heart over the next few years to see where my confidences would lie. It took a lot of prying from these greedy hands before I could slowly surrender my plans for his. He wisely chose not to tell me where he was taking me.

I have a phobia of getting behind. I would have to ward off panic attacks in college when they passed out the semester syllabus. They would never let you get very far ahead, and the weight would stay on my shoulders until the last assignment was crossed off the list. Don't get me wrong. I love lists. I make them just so I can cross things off. I sometimes add things to the list that I just did even though they weren't on the list just so I can cross them off.

I would have three months of the calendar on my refrigerator, and they were usually all full. When I heard that other women didn't necessarily do that, I justified it as a noble thing. *I am a firstborn. I am a perfectionist. I like to be organized, efficient. I'm a type-A personality.* Who was I kidding? Being a control freak is never healthy.

I heard a young pastor say that God did not raise Jesus from the dead to follow *us* around our day. *Ouch.* God must laugh when he has kids like me. There's so much unlearning to do. I tend to have my hour, my day, my week, my month, and yes, my year planned. I was walking with God ... if he could keep up. Oh, the pains he would go to in order to teach me to stay behind the cross. There would be a day coming when I had no calendars on my fridge because I would rarely leave my home.

❦

Every Thanksgiving before dinner, we would share what we were most thankful for during the past year. We might go around the table and just tell one another, or we would distribute scraps of paper, write down recalled blessings, and then share. All I knew was that I wanted to be creative and different each year, but the same thing always came to mind. Besides Jesus and family, I was always overwhelmed with gratitude that I got to stay home with my kids. I have girlfriends who have heard God call them to work outside the home, and they seem to balance their job and family fine. But I just had a passion about being home, and I was so happy that my husband supported that decision. Things just went smoother with me there.

More than anything, Gary and I just wanted our children to walk closely with the Lord after leaving our home and starting life on their own. We were not seeing that happen in some of our friends' children's lives though. That scared us.

We were so proud when our kids learn to bow their heads and pray at two years old. We applauded when they made the decision to be baptized or go with the youth group on a mission trip. But we were seeing a real disconnect among some of their friends during high school when their true faith was coming into question. *What about our children, Lord? How will we navigate if that happens?*

The kids who succeeded during this transition had several things in common. They knew the Word because they had memorized it and studied it. These children were more able to address the questions that college professors would likely throw at them. They also had an outward focus and compassion for others.

Mission trips and community service were usually a crucial part of their training. They understood that there were only two groups—the lost and the saved. Our culture tends to blur these lines.

But the most common denominator in raising kids who would continue in their faith walk was the presence of two parents committed to each other in marriage and committed to loving and trusting the Lord. We saw success when we saw this as a top priority. I have witnessed some amazing exceptions as single parents have leaned on God's grace to allow them to achieve these goals as well.

> These are the commands, decrees and laws the Lord your God directed me to teach you ... so that you, your children and their children after them may fear the Lord your God as long as you live ... Impress them on your children. Talk about them when you sit at home and when you walk along the road, when you lie down and when you get up. Tie them as symbols on your hands and bind them on your foreheads. Write them on the doorframes of your houses and on your gates. (Deuteronomy 6:1–2a, 7–9 NIV)

That takes an intentional investment of time! No one else is going to do that for your child, not the way you can. It's not just quality time. This scripture talks about the quantity that is involved in relationships. I needed them to have the best of me, not the leftovers at the end of the day.

There were opportunities God gave me to earn money while staying at home. When the children were young, I ran a daycare for a while. I gave guitar and gymnastic lessons from our basement, and I did pretty well selling health supplements.

When our kids were a little older, I tried substitute teaching part-time in the local school district. That still caused a little too much chaos in our evenings, so it was short-lived, but I felt free to try. I listened to what the Lord was telling me during my quiet times. His will is tailor-made for us alone. If we are listening, he will make it clear.

Does this atmosphere guarantee that our kids will always live for him? I'm speaking from experience when I say that it does not. We cannot control that as much as we would like to. We are demanded to lay a firm foundation and do all that we can, and even if they walk away for a while, it gives them something to come back to, a solid rock. When one of them chooses to launch out and sow some wild oats, the enemy will see to it that you beat yourself up and drown in guilt. If you know that you have leaned on Christ and made your children's faith walk your priority, it will be easier to trust his sovereignty as he promises to "restore the years the locust hath eaten" (Joel 2:25a AKJV).

———————

As expected, there are compromises. We drove older cars, swapped fine dinners out for picnics, and got pretty creative at Christmas. Our kids learned how much further their allowance went at garage sales, and they knew they weren't getting a phone until they had a job to pay for it. Living financially close also gave them the chance to see God's promises at work since often unforeseen expenses would blindside us.

One Christmas there simply were no funds. We came home one day in early November to find our house had been robbed— TVs, stereos, computers, mostly electronics that we had bought secondhand. Several friends generously shared extras, and then the insurance company gave us full value on everything. Christmas was saved. Thank you, Lord!

Another Christmas came when we needed help. Our car was worth more dead than alive. I seriously suggested to the Lord that I leave it at the edge of the parking lot at the grocery store one weekend while I was in the store with all the children, and then maybe someone could hit it. I was truly disappointed to see it intact when I walked out.

The following Thursday, my oldest daughter burst through the front door of our home and said, "Dad just hit a deer! The deer got up and ran away, but he said the car is totaled."

I jumped up and said, "That'll work, Lord!" With the payoff, we bought a better car and had a wonderful Christmas and wondered if angels ever took the shape of deer.

These close calls were not a lighthearted experience for me. In those early days, nothing was as important as feeling secure. I could make myself sick with worry, and it would spread stress to the whole family. But as these trials continued, God remained faithful. I know because I kept prayer journals, and when the next ordeal would rear its ugly head, Gary and I would go out on the deck and find comfort just reading about his faithfulness over the previous years.

In almost thirty years of raising a family, me working from home and my husband working as a commercial service technician, we have never gone into debt for Christmas. We have always had a vacation, and we have never been late paying a bill. And it is because ... *he is faithful!*

I asked him once if I could tell other women that he would provide for them as well. Or was he just doing this for me? He assured me that I could tell others that such a blessing was for them too. They just need to trust and obey. You just can't beat it. Choose joy while you wait, stand back, and behold the glory of the Lord.

"Though the fig tree does not bud and there are no grapes on the vines, though the olive crop fails and the fields produce no food, though there are no sheep in the pen and no cattle in the stalls, yet I will rejoice in the LORD, I will be joyful in God my Savior" (Habakkuk 3:17–18 NIV).

Gary and I longed for our Christian walk to be utterly dependent on Christ and to "Rejoice in the Lord always. I will say it again: Rejoice!" (Philippians 4:4 NIV). We were not there yet. If we wanted our children to get there, then we would have to learn to stand on that mountain, close our eyes, throw our hands up, and fall back on his promises.

Chapter 2

Preparing the Soil

"Forgive them, Jesus, for they know not what they say!" Nothing reveals your true doctrine like the comforting words you choose to use to encourage others during a crisis. For two weeks, our young daughter Emily was fighting for her life after coming down with spinal meningitis on Christmas Eve. Using the old mercury thermometer, we saw the line go all the way to the top, and so we raced to the local hospital.

Sincere friends flooded us with idioms. *It's God's will. All things work together for good. Keep good thoughts. I know how you are feeling.* But the one that always gave me more guilt than comfort was when people said, "You've just got to have faith."

I get it. That awkward moment when your heart and mind are not in sync and out comes some careless verbiage. It's too late to suck it back in, so you hope that their grief will mask the actual words and that they'll get the gist of the message as you scoot out the door. But what does that saying mean? Faith in what?

Faith that she will not die? He doesn't promise that. Faith that it will be over soon? He doesn't guarantee that either. How about that there will be no permanent damage? Nope. So what ground does our faith land on in times like this?

I remember taking the family to see *Peter Pan* one holiday

season. Afterward, the girls chanted for the next few weeks, "I do believe in fairies! I do! I do!" It was like if you said it loud and strong enough with your eyes closed, they would appear. Is that what faith is? Name it and claim it loudly. Do we only focus on good thoughts, drown out any negativity, and refuse to hear anything that suggest things will not turn out the way that we prayed?

I loved the story my mom shared with me when I was a young wife. She knew my temperament all too well. A father drove his car through a snowstorm to pick up his mother-in-law and his young son, whom she had been babysitting. He was bringing them both back to the house to share a meal. After greeting his dad, his son curled up in the backseat and fell asleep while the grandma climbed in next to the boy. She was terrified of the storm and leaned over the front seat, directing and scolding the driver all the way to his house. When they arrived safely, the little boy woke up, and both passengers got out. Then my mom asked me, "Who had more faith, the little boy or the grandma?"

Of course, I answered the little boy, and she quickly tipped her head as if asking, "Are you sure that is your final answer?" She then replied, "They both had faith. They both got in the car. Only one enjoyed the ride more."

I have played that example out so many times in my head over the last few decades. Faith is obeying. "By faith Abraham, when called to go to a place he would later receive as his inheritance, obeyed and went, even though he did not know where he was going" (Hebrews 11:8 NIV).

It's not dictating to God loudly where you would like this experience to go and then thinking it's faith to hold him to it. It's letting him lead you by your right hand even though you don't know where he is taking you. It's okay to be scared and anxious and trembling at times. I found those feelings changed the older I got and the more roads he and I traveled together.

I also am now able to enjoy the ride more. I used to visualize walking with God while resting in the palm of his hand. Something would happen not to my liking, and I could see myself jumping up and down, hanging off the side of his hand or biting his thumb. Then he would simply stop, open his hand, and stare at me as if to kindly ask, "Are you finished?" I would then lie back down, huffing and puffing, totally out of breath. He would gently close his hand around me and continue walking, never noticing that I was exhausted, not to mention embarrassed.

"So faith comes from hearing, and hearing through the word of Christ" (Romans 10:17 ESV). I have learned that nothing replaces being in God's Word daily. As you hear it, you learn his promises. I have learned to let my faith land on his promises. So with Emily's illness, what were the promises that I could have claimed?

"But my God shall supply all your need according to his riches in glory by Christ Jesus" (Philippians 4:19 KJV). I knew he would provide gas somehow to make the trip back and forth to the hospital. I knew he would help with a babysitter for Blaine. I knew he would help us pay the doctor bill. I knew we would not miss a meal during this time and that all of our other bills would be paid, even though my husband was missing work.

"For he grants sleep to those he loves" (Psalm 127:2 NIV). "I call to remembrance, my song in the night" (Psalm 77:6 AKJV). "When you lie down, you will not be afraid" (Proverbs 3:24a NIV). I could claim by faith that he wanted me to have a good night's rest without fear.

"And we know that in all things God works for the good of those who love him, who have been called according to his purpose" (Romans 8:28 NIV). "But he knows the way that I take and when he has tested me, I will come forth as gold" (Job 23:10 NIV). He knows! He knows! He has a plan. He has a purpose. He knows what he's doing. And we don't have to see where we are going or understand the path! And how would you grasp all of these things if you didn't know what his Word says?

Yes, faith is always the answer, but faith in what and who? What promises are you claiming? Find them. Have a trusted friend help you. Let your faith land on God's firm foundation, and watch your trust soar.

For my birthday one year, I received a nonfiction historical account of the ghost towns and graveyards in the Rockies titled *Ghost Towns of the West*. The person who gave me the gift obviously knew me well and was not surprised that I read it cover to cover. In college I did a term paper on the exact subject. I loved hearing about the small towns that popped up during the mining years in Colorado and the wild, infamous characters that were buried in the local cemeteries.

On trips out west, I would seek out the sites I had learned about, usually only known by the locals. Visiting the Rosita graveyard near Westcliffe, Colorado, was especially satisfying. This town had gone up against Denver for the state capital and lost by two votes. The silver mines all dried up in the area, and the town is now a quick drive-by at best.

I traveled a long way up one of the mountains in the Sangre De Cristo range to get to this particular cemetery, first driving and then on foot. Now seeing those wrought-iron gates barely visible through the trees made my heart pound and excitement soar! The gates swung open as I gently tugged at them. I felt like tiptoeing on the pine needle carpet below me. It was so quiet—except for the wind in the pines. It was eerily, hauntingly quiet.

More iron gates outlined the sunken graves. If I stood near them long enough, a story would often unfold. A mother lying next to her newborn, neither surviving childbirth. Thank you, Lord, for hospitals. Several young siblings dying within days of one another. Thank you, Lord, for vaccines. The average age of death for an adult was in their forties. Mountain life was a hard life.

Most mining towns had no churches but a dozen saloons. Often the town was lawless, and I enjoyed coming across the graves of some of the rowdy bunch I had read about. One tombstone went into detail about a miner dying after his dynamite exploded while he slept. It had frozen, and he was letting it thaw by the fire.

What did the people standing around during the burial look like? What were they wearing? How do you go on after losing several children or your wife and baby on the day you should be celebrating? Did they have hope? Did they know the Lord?

Before I had children, I had a friend who would accommodate me by taking a sack lunch and going to the local cemetery. It was such a peaceful place to reflect and think about heaven. I liked reading headstones to try to figure out if the person knew Jesus.

When I was coaching high school sports, I took my girls' volleyball team to a graveyard during a lull in an out-of-state tournament. We made it a scavenger hunt, looking for the oldest, the youngest, and the one with the longest or shortest name. We would try to find the largest family or guess the cause of death. But I always had them looking for evidence about where this person was spending eternity. Later with my family, we would study a little about the history of the vacation area we would be visiting, find the local graveyard, and do the same thing. We collected some of the epitaphs that stood out, sad and happy.

While watching my husband play softball in a rural Kansas

town, I spotted a small number of graves in a field beyond the diamond and across two railroad tracks. The graves were from the 1880s, the height of the wild west. Once again, a mom and baby had died together, Sadie Bell Rose and Lizzie Kate. Don't those names fit that era perfectly? I just loved finding those sweet graves.

Another time we were wading in a creek way out in the sticks of northern Arkansas on a very hot August day. This place was in the middle of nowhere! I saw a cluster of pines up on a nearby hill and figured there were graves beneath it. I put my flip-flops back on and began hiking alone up through this meadow. I was right. It was a family plot, and the epitaph I would read was so moving that I recorded it in the back of my Bible. It was a tombstone from the late 1800s of a young girl who had left this life at just eighteen years old.

> Plucked from the blossom of her youth,
> Here to rot in the dust forever more.

No hope. So telling. So sad.

A beautiful contrast would be found up in the military cemetery at Fort Leavenworth in Kansas. A twelve-year-old boy had preceded his parents that now lay on either side of him. Their faith was sure. I knelt to my knees, reading the epitaph.

> "What I do, thou knowest not now,
> but thou shalt know thereafter."
> —John 13:7

Oh, the hope that's found in Christ! What security we have in his love! We have the peace knowing that even when a sparrow falls, "Yet, not one of them will fall to the ground outside your Father's care" (Matthew 10:29b NIV).

The truth is we do rot in the dust, not just forevermore. Like any seed tucked away in the prepared soil, we will rot, shed our old casings to allow new life to burst forth, springing from this earth. And for those of us that know Jesus, "And so shall we ever be with the Lord" (1 Thessalonians 4:17b KJV).

But it's not just at death that we experience this. Paul says, "Therefore we do not lose heart. Though outwardly we are wasting away, yet inwardly we are being renewed day by day" (2 Corinthians 4:16 NIV). What soil does God have you buried in these days? Is it bad health, surmounting bills, or watching kids make bad choices? He wants to begin to break that old shell even while we are still underground.

If you walk with him long enough, then you know the routine. You get back to practicing the disciplines of the faith again—counting your blessings, giving thanks, surrendering to the moment, taking time in the Word, getting on your knees, practicing obedience, and meditating. "I think of you through the watches of the night" (Psalm 63:6b NIV). We know what it takes to abide in Christ, and when you begin, it doesn't take long before we begin to die to self. Those chains begin to fall off, and we are movin' on up!

Actually, *dying to self* used to feel like I had to give up my desires and dreams to serve him. Like I was relinquishing my identity and even personality to become a puppet or a zombie. It felt like I was a slave on the auction block saying goodbye to the only life and fun I had known. "But if suffering for Jesus was the lot I must live, then so be it."

I was so far off! He asks me to trade in my sorrows for his joy, and he will help me "to loose the chains of the injustice, and untie the cords of the yoke, to set the oppressed free and break every yoke" (Isaiah 58:6b NIV). "Then you will find your joy in the Lord, and I will cause you to ride in triumph on the heights of the land and feast on the inheritance of your father Jacob. For the mouth of the Lord has spoken" (Isaiah 58:14 NIV).

I love the word *steadfast* found in scripture. That's probably because I am not. When you are not *steadfast*, then you are easily tossed around by waves, so … you become afraid of *waves*. And there are a lot of them out there. They are the unknown forces, usually not on your calendar, that threaten to knock you off your feet and rob you of sleep.

After just not feeling well for six months, I wound up in the hospital, where I underwent a gamut of tests to try to come up with a diagnosis. Three days on ice chips only and hurting from head to toe, they wheeled me down to take yet another test. I was to be tied down on a gurney and asked not to move for two hours. You might as well have tarred and feathered me! I did not think I could survive it.

I knew it would take the Lord intervening. I asked him to help me remember all the "fear not" verses I could think of. Because of my severe headache, I asked him to knock me out so I could sleep, but mostly, I sang all the songs I could think of that mentioned *waves*. Christian radio was full of them, and it was a great distraction.

I love Bethel's song "You Make Me Brave," and I would say that line over and over. It goes on to remind us that God calls us out from the safety of the shore to come out and trust him in the waves.

Our faith doesn't typically grow when we are sitting comfortably on the beach all the time. We cannot know true peace living in an Adirondack chair. Oswald Chambers writes in *My Utmost for His Highest*, "Faith must be tested, because it can be turned into a personal possession only through conflict."

I survived the test. My surgeon came in early Sunday morning and said simply that I had no stones. My gallbladder just wasn't working. He also said, "I am aware that this is not only Mother's Day but your birthday as well and that you are missing out on a big party at home." He suggested I check out, go home, and return in a few days. He would take care of the problem in outpatient. I could have kissed his feet. Thank you, Lord!

You know, sometimes the waves can be really fun. After all, who takes an ocean-side vacation and chooses to stay on the beach the whole time?

One Monday, we received in the mail an anonymous gift in the amount of $1,000. The note attached simply said, "We love you." First, we were shocked. Then we were jubilant. Then we were suspicious.

We wondered what the Lord was preparing us for. Nothing urgent was going on at the time, but we have seen him give us provision ahead of time, not just during or after a need. So thinking we might not use it to celebrate quite yet, we put it up on the refrigerator. We then shared it with the kids so they could enjoy our fun dilemma and watch for God to work.

My husband had been struggling at work lately. An illness had sidelined the owner, and a temporary replacement had been brought in to run the company. Gary had been frustrated with some of the changes, and some confrontations had taken place. Every night I could see the stress that he was under. I had been reading Genesis, and I told him some of the scriptures were perfect for what he was going through. We went out on the deck and read Jacob's account with Laban.

"So Jacob sent word to Rachel and Leah. He said to them, 'I see that your father's attitude toward me is not what it was before, but the God of my father has been with me. You know that I've worked for your father with all my strength, yet your father has cheated me by changing my wages ten times. However, God has not allowed him to harm me'" (Genesis 31:4a, 5–7 NIV). "The angel of God said to me in the dream ... I have seen all that Laban has been doing to you" (Genesis 31: 11a, 12b NIV).

Gary called me one Friday evening to say the new boss wanted to talk with him. When Gary still wasn't home at 9:00 p.m., I knew something was wrong. I headed to my bedroom and got down on my knees to pray for him. A short time later, I opened my eyes and just knew why he was late. He was getting fired, and that check on the fridge was for groceries. He walked in a half hour later, pale as a ghost, and for the first time in his life, he had been fired for insubordination. I quickly ran and hugged him, told him I knew, and reminded him of the provision in the kitchen.

I was not working. He was carrying the full load, so this news devastated him. He worried so much about getting hired when he now would have a firing on his resume. We decided not to think about it the next day, Saturday, but to give it to the Lord and just breathe.

The following day was Sunday, and we both came home alone from church as our kids stayed to help with the worship band. We were both praying on our knees at our loveseat when Gary stopped and jumped up and started dialing a respected man he knew who ran a similar company. He was going to simply ask a couple of questions about going into business for himself.

When the owner heard what had happened to Gary, he told him that he had a briefcase full of job applications that he had not had time to go through. He admired Gary's work and would love for him to come to work for him at the same pay and offered overtime. The problem was he couldn't hire him for a week because he needed that time to get him tools, uniforms, and a truck. But he said that he would be ready for Gary a week from tomorrow.

I was still on my knees when I saw Gary hang up the phone, hang his head, and start to cry. I had never seen that before. He walked over, hugged me, and said that this was the biggest answer to prayer that God had ever done for him. The check on the refrigerator would easily carry us that next week.

How fun it was to share the news when the kids came barging through the door a couple of hours later. Sometimes it's too much to put our stresses on the children, but in this instance, we were glad they got to see God's provision. We did not miss one day of income. That job would carry him to retirement, and the former job went under shortly after he left. God is good ... all the time.

Despite all of the decaying and death-defying flurry going on underground to planted seeds, the garden is still my favorite place to be in the spring. After a good rain and a few sunny days, you will find me on my knees, gently pulling back leaves and mulch, searching for the first green evidence of life. Thank you, Lord, for seasons. And isn't it interesting that even the plants and trees need rainy days *and* sunny days to be healthy. Do we need any less?

"There is a time for everything, and a season for every activity under the heavens: a time to plant and a time to uproot, a time to weep and a time to laugh, a time to mourn and a time to dance" (Ecclesiastes 3:1, 2b, 4).

We live for the harvest, and we rarely struggle with faulty emotions or lousy attitudes during this time of celebration. The holidays, graduations, new babies, and vacations are all God's blessings and a time to laugh and have fun! "Bless the Lord, who daily loadeth us with benefits, even the God of our salvation" (Psalm 68:19 KJV). Amen ... and I am all about having fun!

For me, the struggle comes during the waiting. The longer the wait, the harder I have to work to remain good company. But knowing that he's *here*, that he *knows*, and that everything that happens to me is filtered through his hand gives me peace. *Hope springs eternal.*

So the next time someone tells you, "You've just got to have faith," you just smile ... and enjoy the ride.

Chapter 3

A Tough Row to Hoe

When I became a mom, my journey of faith shifted to an outward focus. That makes sense. Your children's lives become more important than your own. Satan knows that too. Mama Bear soon surfaces and says, "Mess with my kids, and you mess with me."

I'm embarrassed when I visualize my role as mom during the early years. I am out in front of the whole family, crouched like a ninja, holding my breath and wielding my sword. In one way, it seems noble, but it's exhausting!

What is the balance? This noun became the "B" word in our household because it was the answer to just about everything. Solomon says, "Whoever fears God will avoid all extremes" (Ecclesiastes 7:18b NIV). I began seeking God at a deeper level during this time of my life simply because I lacked the wisdom to know *balance*.

When the garden plants begin popping up in the spring, so do the weeds. If I don't do my least favorite task, the hoeing, on a regular basis, then I can't distinguish between the two. Soon the plants are choked out or become weak and unproductive at the very least. What do I protect my children from, and what do I let make them stronger?

Having shade only keeps most plants from flourishing, but sun alone can scorch them. Surprisingly, droughts can make the roots stronger as they grow deeper to seek water, but fertilizer, which is meant to increase growth, can also burn plants if too much is given. Some wind is necessary for pollination, but strong winds can uproot the plant. Ah! Raising children is not for the faint of heart!

You can't look to culture for the balance. Nor can you base your morals on the ever-pivoting, relative thinking of this age. My former pastor once said that whenever you hear the word *kingdom* in the Bible, think of the word *culture*. So when Jesus prays to the Father, "Your kingdom come, your will be done, on earth as it is in heaven" (Matthew 6:10 NIV), he wants the culture of heaven to be here on earth. Ultimately, it will be, but for now we are to fight for it at every turn.

This convicted me to be a room mother, join the PTA, get involved with politics, and follow current events. We can be culturally relative without wallowing in it. Billy Graham reminds us, "Be in the world but not of it."

If I ever came back at my mom and said, "All the kids are doing it," I would be reminded, "Other kids may, but you may not. You were bought with a price." It really never occurred to me that she would be persuaded, but I would try now and again. Eventually, I had that conviction myself, and it got easier to line myself up with what God would have me do. That's where I wanted my children to be. What if they didn't want to be there?

One of the sweet surprises of moving to our rural home came when I met our closest neighbor. Terree was a smart, confident, tiny thing who loved God, her six-foot-four husband and three school-age children. She was ahead of me in homeschooling and 4-H and willing to help me get started. She had a passion for learning, way ahead of her time in homesteading, herbal homeopathic living, and the sciences. She was a whiz at nutritional cooking and an accomplished seamstress, and she agreed to be my mentor! I never felt jealous of her. I always saw her as a blessing.

Terree succumbed to cancer a few years later and left everyone stunned. She was the center of so many people's world. A thousand people were at her funeral, hearing the gospel and the hope that she had in Christ. Every car that headed to the graveside had a balloon on it, and it felt like the parade went on forever.

I remember worshipping in church a couple of days later. Heaven had never seemed so real to me as it did then. I sat there thinking, *She still exists. She's just not my neighbor anymore. But she will be again someday.* Oh, the reality of eternity when someone you love goes there.

Terree's youngest child, Thomas, was seven and best friends with my six-year-old son, Reed. The last year she was sick, we began including Thomas in all of our family activities. Her other two children were older and could manage with their dad still working.

Terree was passionate about homeschooling, and I told her I would look after that as well. He went on vacation and camping trips with us, and he enjoyed holidays and school with my kids. Eventually, he became part of our family.

We had the privilege of watching him grow, and I homeschooled him through his senior year. And then we helped him pursue his dream in the US Marines. God blessed his dad and siblings, and they survived the sadness and sorrow. They continued to walk with their Savior and to serve him in their communities.

The next surprise was Maisie. She was my chatter-box niece who, because of family circumstances, would need to come live with us just short of the next eleven years. She would reach less than five feet at full height, but she could hold her own with any of her *new* brothers. We were now at six plus Gary's two grown sons. We would soon be facing the whirlwind of five teenagers at once. Bring it on!

"Train up a child in the way he should go, and even when he is old he will not depart from it" (Proverbs 22:6 KJV). That proverb is a powerhouse of wisdom! How do we know the "way they should go?" *We now have eight children with seven different mothers. They all have different gifts, talents, dreams, strengths, weaknesses, personalities, health profiles, and backgrounds. Do I just throw everything at them and see what sticks?*

We started with consistent prayer when they were in my tummy or when they first came to us. We prayed that they would all come to the Lord at an early age. We asked that they have a healthy fear of the Lord and that they have wisdom. I came across a wonderful scripture in the life of King David concerning the subject of wisdom in our kid's lives.

We know the story of Solomon being visited by God, who told him, "Ask for whatever you want me to give you." Solomon replied, "Give me wisdom and knowledge that I may lead these people well" (2 Chronicles 1: 7, 10 NIV). Before this happened though, David called Solomon to have a word with him. "Now, my son, the Lord be with you and may you have success and build the house of the Lord your God, as he said you would. May the Lord give you discretion and understanding when he puts you in command over Israel, so that you may keep the law of the Lord your God" (1 Chronicles 22:11, 12 NIV).

David prayed for his son to have discretion and understanding, and when offered a choice by God later, Solomon asked for wisdom and knowledge. God had gone ahead and interceded. That showed me the power of a praying parent and the need to ask for help to "lead my children well."

I remember that my mom seemed to choose her ministry in life based on whatever seasons we were going through as children. During our middle school, she would have Bible clubs after school in our home. During our junior high, she became a youth coach, and when we were in high school, it was nothing to have dozens of our friends over on a Thursday night to study the Bible for a couple of hours.

Our home was always open to teenagers. Well, almost always. We had a sign on our front door that said, "If you are high or drunk, you can't come in." Foosball was popular in the '70s, and if you wanted to get in on tournaments, the only place to play was at local bar on our town square called The Hole in the Wall, where drugs and drink were a part of the scene.

My mom was able to get a hold of a professional foosball table to encourage kids to come to our home instead. At my tenth high school reunion, an old friend came up and let me know that he had trudged all across town in the snow to come over and play foosball, but he read the sign and had to turn around and head back. He let me know he was not happy!

My mom didn't mess around. I can't tell you how many bags of marijuana she flushed down our toilet. I saw kids cry as they watched it swirl away. They all knew she loved them though, and many kids came to Christ at our home during the revival of the '70s because of her.

I tried to follow her lead and involve my kids in most of

my activities as well. It wasn't easy. Trying to serve the Lord in ministry can make you feel like a wishbone going for a ride. You are pulled in directions you don't want to go. I had a deacon firmly come up to me and say the Lord told him that I was to be on his committee. Well, God didn't tell me, and I learned to guard my time after that. God pressed on my heart that my children were the *one thing.* Everything else right now was secondary.

If I took charge of the building of the parade float, they were stuffing tissue paper in chicken wire right beside me. If I was running the Fall Hoedown, they were carving pumpkins, helping me hang lights in the barn, and picking out fiddle music. As young adults, they told me that these were some of their best memories, and they now felt confident to help and even lead in their own home churches.

"These commandments that I give you today are to be on your hearts. Impress them on your children. Talk about them when you sit at home and when you walk along the road, when you lie down and when you get up" (Deuteronomy 6:6–7 NIV).

In the scope of their whole lives, I had such a small block of time to influence and shape them before they left my care. Truth is that I just enjoyed and loved being with them. You will have so much time to fill when they leave, and most of those service opportunities are not lost forever. They will just be different. Redeem the days now, my friend.

As moms chitchat over coffee, sharing their lives and loves, a common theme often slips into the conversation, namely guilt. They feel guilty for taking the time for coffee when there are "places to go, people to see, and things to do." Or maybe it's guilt over spending five dollars on your grande white mocha caramel skinny latte, hold the whip. But mostly, what I find is that young women feel most guilty about their hectic schedules, which prevent them from doing everything a *good mom* should do.

I recall unloading on my mom about the conflicting agendas as a new school year was approaching. She simply said that she felt sorry for young women today. She commented that because she didn't have all my choices, it was just easier. And she didn't see that having more gave me peace or joy.

Women raising their families in the 1950s are scoffed at now, and yes, we are blessed with *some* better choices; however, there is something to be said for the simplicity their life afforded them. If you went into a fine restaurant and instead of being handed a menu, you were given a large bound book to order from, how would you react? I can wear myself out shopping in a big-box store because there are too many choices. I read all of the labels, trying to get the best for my family, and then I don't get out of there for two hours!

Now that grandkids are entering the picture, I'm surprised that I don't often get asked for advice and wisdom in parenting them. But why would I? Our kids have volumes and volumes of advice at their fingertips on any given search engine! And we know if it's on the Internet, it's true, right?

It is a lie that we can have it all. Maybe here and there, but not all at once. If you're spread too thin, no one gets the best you have to offer. The problem for me is that when I try to slow down, set priorities, and regroup, usually on a Monday, it lasts for only a few days. Usually, I will get sidelined by some bubble bath commercial or Hallmark movie and tell myself that I deserve some *me* time. Where's the *B* word? *Balance* is everything.

Tucked away in my Bible, I keep a note I wrote to myself on a day I was definitely not balanced.

Secret, Unspoken Thoughts

This day wasted my talent.
I was created for more than being a referee, chauffer and maid.
These children are holding me back
from using my gifts and wisdom
to accomplish world changing events.
I secretly believe my name should be
up in lights somewhere.
My family doesn't appreciate my sacrifices
and these non-eternal annoyances
are wasting my time.
They are detouring me from my true calling,
... and today, that irritates me.
But ... life is made up of ordinary days and how I choose
to face those days says everything about my character.
Lord, help me to look for you in the mundane.

—*Carole*

I wanted our home to be an oasis for my family, a resort, a place to retreat and rewind. I wanted an escape from the world, our own secret garden. So how did chaos and tension continually creep in? Where was the peace and rest? Why was I raising my voice? Jesus, am I left to figure this all out on my own and come to you only with the big things? The truth is that the happiest people I know live as though God is involved in every detail of their lives. "The steps of a good man are ordered by the Lord" (Psalm 37:23a KJV). "Seek His will in all you do, and he will show you which path to take" (Proverbs 3:6 NLT). "A man's heart plans his way, but the Lord directs his steps" (Proverbs 16:9 NKJV).

God ordering your steps is pretty detailed. I decided he could order my schedule as well. First, it meant seeking him every morning and simply asking him to help me. Was I willing to buck the world's culture and stand alone at times to keep the peace? This would not be easy.

Before I had children, my best friend had four. They were good-looking, smart, and all athletic boys leading their sports teams to championships. I remember she felt like their pace was out of control and decided to take a summer off with no sports. Their coaches were all over them, criticizing, bashing their motives, assuring them they would fall behind and not be able to get scholarships in school. They did it anyway and had the best summer of their school years. The boys never missed a beat, never fell behind, and my friend got her family back.

We realized we could not allow any of our children to become a "jack of all trades." They could not choose to become an expert in every activity that our community offered. There was simply not the time or money. The Lord helped us find and cultivate the gifts that he gave them.

After watching our oldest daughter's violin recital, we decided sports might be the way to go. When our youngest daughter needed help running the bases after hitting the ball off the tee and was crying as she crossed home plate, we bought her a piano. After listening to another young child sing, we handed her a sketch pad. As adults now, these are the areas that they are still excelling in.

God will whittle the fluff away and help us become more intentional and precise when we give him our day and then turn over the calendar as well. We can confidently know that he will lead us to know how to raise each child in the *way he should go* if we ask, are willing to listen, and surrender the reins to his loving care.

Our kids will not catch our love for the Lord through osmosis. It takes hard, intentional work, but it can be fun. If you don't have Christian radio, you can save up money to go to concerts or buy Christian CDs. For Christmas presents, take a trip to the bookstore and let everyone pick out a devotional reading for that year.

Rent or buy Christian movies and have a party. Be the fun house. Make it always available for their friends. Host small groups in your home. Get someone else to facilitate it if you're not comfortable.

Go on field trips to hear motivational speakers and stop for pizza afterward. Times spent at summer camps make up some of the best childhood memories for adults. Get involved with good youth groups, and learn how to serve in your community. Serve with them. Help them find their spiritual gifts so that they can find the best area to serve in. Get them grounded in apologetics so they can defend themselves during the college years. Help them learn to sing or play an instrument so they can get involved with a worship band.

By far the best activity for giving our children an outward focus and a biblical worldview was going on mission trips. We found a wonderful ministry that specialized in teaching children to serve through community outreach and world missions. When they travel internationally, they tend to come back with more patriotism, more gratitude, and more brokenness for the lost. This experience will mature a selfish teenager more quickly than anything I know.

The first year each child went on a mission trip, they were allowed to write letters to family and friends, asking for help with raising their financial support. After that, they had to earn it themselves by collecting items for a massive garage sale we would have every spring. We always had a very large figure to raise with multiple children going, but every year they would see God's faithfulness as it always came in.

We would not price the items but instead asked for donations in the amount they thought the items were worth. The kids would put up flyers and posters explaining their mission, and they were able to witness for Christ at the same time. I loved meeting all of our rural neighbors every spring.

We found we doubled our income compared to just marking everything with a tag. People usually wanted to help when they understood the cause. It was a lot of work! We made a lot of trips all over town with the pickup truck. Short on space, we only had a path to walk through our house for a month before the sale.

One year we were $20 short of our goal and just knew we had miscounted. Pretty soon a neighbor came down the driveway, waving a $20 bill, saying she missed the sale but wanted to contribute. I can still see my kids smiling as they all glanced at one another. We would try to mention to buyers that anything left after the sale was free on Sunday. Be careful though. We came home from church to people hauling our patio furniture off the deck. Ha! You try to be nice!

After thirty years of working with teenagers as a youth coach and teacher, I continued to see the same pattern forming in the children who would later walk with God and continue to serve him. Their parents were very involved. They didn't leave it to the Sunday school teacher or youth leader. They were sacrificing time, money, and energy to invest in their kid's spiritual future. They were purpose-driven when it counted, and it paid off.

From time to time, I listen as parents lament their personal struggles in life and vow to give their children easier journeys than they had. I would always feel sad at their regret and their longing for their children to be less of a failure than they were.

What do I really want for my child? Do I see my struggles as a failure? Should my life be focused on steering my family around every danger that I faced?

The turmoil in my life has caused me to seek God, first for survival and then out of gratitude for his mercy. A toddler first obeys to avoid the pain of punishment. It is only later that I felt my children wanting to obey because of the love relationship we had. Well, most of the time.

"We can rejoice, too, when we run into problems and trials, for we know that they help us develop endurance. And endurance develops strength of character, and character strengthens our confident hope of salvation. And this hope will not lead to disappointment. For we know how dearly God loves us" (Romans 5:3–5 NLT).

We want our children to be strong, to have endurance and character, but what do we usually ask for in our prayers? Protection, protection, protection. No! I want my children to go on for the Lord. If my kids love the Lord as much as I do when they are adults, I will be very happy. But look what it has taken for me to get here! I doubt you can know him fully without conflict in your life. Chuck Swindoll says, "Never trust a man that doesn't limp." If I am looking for a mentor, I look for the scars.

In the classic novel from the 1970s *Hinds Feet in High Places*, Hannah Hurnard writes allegorically of a faith journey from a nonbeliever to an immature believer to an abiding believer. The young girl is named Much Afraid, and she is on a journey from the Valley of Humiliation to the mountaintop called the High Places of the Shepherd.

I read this as a teenager, and my most vivid memory was her fear of the two companions the shepherd had given her for her venture, Sorrow and Suffering. She refused their offer to help in the beginning even when the path was full of obstacles; however, when the mountain became steep, she had no choice but to cling to them, and somehow the journey was made easier. When she allowed them to work with her she became stronger and more sure-footed.

Don't let me refuse your help, Lord. How vain I would be had I pulled myself up by my own bootstraps. How independent I would remain if all my wisdom led to success and promotion. How would I ever know true peace without you? I might be happy, but would I know joy? To not live the surrendered life is to live in sin. "To the sinner he gives the task of gathering and storing up wealth to hand it over to the one who pleases God. This too is meaningless, a chasing after the wind" (Ecclesiastes 2:26 NIV).

Lord, spare our children's lives, but do whatever it takes for them to walk with you. You are for them, not against them. Help me remember you love my children more than I do. You know them better than I do. You created them in their inmost being. You knitted them together in their mother's womb. They are fearfully and wonderfully made (Psalm 139).

You know the number of hairs on their heads and the number of days they will live. May they live for you. Use me to help that happen, and should they not choose to follow you in my way or in my time, quiet this mother's heart. Help me remember that your ways are best. Please remind me that you never quit hearing our prayers or quit working on their behalf. I know that I will pick them up and that I will have to do this again, Lord, but today I lay them at your feet.

Chapter 4

Foxes in the Vineyard

"Catch for us the foxes, the little foxes that ruin the vineyards, our vineyards that are in bloom" (Song of Solomon 2:15 NIV). These lies that we believe about God are the "little foxes" that ruin a growing vineyard, a growing relationship with Christ. And notice the foxes come when the garden is in bloom. When I am trying to grow in my faith for Christ, I become a target of the enemy.

One summer I joined some gals in a small group Bible study at a friend's home to study Craig Groeschel's book titled *The Christian Atheist: Believing in God But Living as though He Doesn't Exist.* I would later go on to teach this study to a different group of women at church and then to twenty-five college students in my home. At one point in the study, he asks the group which struggle they related to more—believing that God could love someone as bad as them or believing God could love someone as insignificant as them.

A hundred percent of the women in each group, including me, said they felt more insignificant. This insight was so surprising to me as so many of my friends seemed so confident. What a lie from Satan! Turns out convincing people that God loves them is not their greatest need.

I started with myself and decided to work from the inside out in hope of helping other women. Where was this coming from? My vision of a father was getting his attention during commercial breaks and having something redeeming to show him for intruding. I was to be succinct, quick, and to the point.

Some trophy or medal I had received would be a worthy interruption. Showing him how my first pink lipstick looked, I found out, was not. After I married, I made attempts to call him, and he would answer, "Carole who?" emphasizing his annoyance about how long it had been since I had called.

Is it wrong to transfer your earthly experience of a father onto your heavenly Father? It's a natural jump if it's all you've known. For years, I saw God as the ruling, iron-fisted overseer of my life. I knew he loved me in a *God so loved the world* sort of way. But to stand there and face him alone, see him smile at me, and tell me that he loved me would make me so uncomfortable! I suspected prayers were answered in my life because my mom had prayed, not because I did. I saw him holding a baseball bat and asking, "Where have you been? It's been three days since I last heard from you!"

As much as I struggled with feeling that I was unconditionally loved, the feeling of being insignificant or unworthy was even stronger. The older I got, the more sins piled up and the more trophies and medals I needed to balance it all. Seeking value, I became unbalanced in *doing*, not just *being*. I was active in everything, serving on boards and always taking some *continuing education* class on the side. Keeping up with myself was exhausting. My poor family.

Because I have the privilege of working with young women, I know that many of them are afraid that if others really knew them, these people wouldn't like them. They feel they are falling short of pleasing God on a daily basis, often wondering if they are of any use to him. Most of them relate to Martha rather than Mary in the gospel story that parallels learning to serve rather than sitting at Jesus's feet. Once again, it's the struggle of *doing* verses just *being.*

"By grace are you saved through faith, and that not of yourself, it is the gift of God, not of works lest any man should boast" (Ephesians 2:8–9 KJV). We know our salvation is not based on our works, but we sometimes wonder if our answered prayers, ability to be used, and the joy of pleasing him is based on works. I realize disobedience can hinder all of those areas, but that's not what these women are worried about that is causing this dread of uselessness.

"The tendency today is to put the emphasis on service. Beware of the people who make usefulness their ground of appeal. The lodestar of the saint is God Himself, not estimated usefulness" (Oswald Chambers). I have spent my whole adult life learning what this really means, learning that my relationship is more valuable to God than my service.

We want to be needed, to be essential to the body of Christ. His Word says that we are. He has equipped each of us with talents, gifts, and abilities to be a vital part of his church, but the "accuser of the brethren," Satan, is bent on making us feel worthless. That is why we must know his promises to keep the voices of untruth at bay.

I remember learning about Elijah spending a considerable amount of time by himself at a place God had called him to. Before the miracle on Mount Carmel, God brought him to the *Kerith Ravine*, which means to "cut or whittle down."

> So, he did what the Lord had told him. He went to
> the Kerith Ravine, east of the Jordan, and stayed
> there. The ravens brought him bread and meat in

the morning and bread and meat in the evening, and he drank from the brook. Sometime later the brook dried up because there had been no rain in the land. Then the word of the Lord came to him: Go at once. (1 Kings 17:5–9 NIV)

How could he be pleasing the Lord by doing nothing, not even preparing his own meals or drawing water? When I was young, I knew there must be a hidden message in all of this, but I just didn't get it. It didn't even really seem like he was on a training expedition, more like a vacation. I was stronger than that, didn't need a rest. He must have just been old.

Convincing myself to just get busy serving sometimes left me feeling empty. I could order my day, make my lists, serve my Savior, but at the end of the day, I was still wondering if it was enough. *Where was the joy?*

One pastor asked us to think of a question that we would ask Jesus if we had a chance to sit down with him one-on-one. Mine was "Am I pleasing you?" The enemy would continually tell me no.

The time for raising children was the area where doubt plagued me the most. I was constantly trying to keep margins in my life. You know, that important space around the edges. I was always striving to figure out how full my plate could be.

Most of my friends worked and raised children. I was never really a crowd follower, but I was constantly checking in with the Lord just to make sure I was on the path he laid out for me. When he would make his will clear to me, it really helped for me to write it down in the form of a personal letter from Jesus to me.

A Letter from God—Nov. 2

*Good morning! I love you and have a wonderful day
planned for you. Even though it seems routine, I have a lot
of hidden blessings throughout the day. Look for them! I
will bring people in your life to encourage you and for you
to encourage. It's your spiritual gift! Watch for them!
I know that you are trying to be the best mom and wife that
you can be. I see that you've given up a career to be home with
your children. This is what I have chosen for you. I see you make
small decisions to please me throughout the day but wonder
about your motives sometimes. Just tell me about them and
then move on. I see you trying not to worry about the future,
replacing anxious thought with scripture and then continuing
on. That's what I want you to do. I'll take care of things.
I see you trying to grow in my Word but always feeling
guilty about not spending enough time with me. Just enjoy
being in my presence, not always doing. I just like being
with you, and I'm glad you take me everywhere.
I see you talking to your children about me constantly. Thank
you for taking them to church and youth group. Thank you for
buying them music about me. I really do hear you every time you
cry out to me about them. I love them more than you do, and
I have a plan for each of them. They are my responsibility.
I have granted you grace in your marriage and have forgiven
your past. I want you and Gary to have a strong, spiritual
relationship because I'm going to use you to help others.
I will bless your relationship as you both seek me.
Now go have a wonderful day! Smile and choose to be happy.
This is the day I have made, choose to rejoice and be glad in it.
I love you, and I am proud of you.
—Jesus
PS You do please me.*

That is 180 degrees different than anything I have ever heard from my earthly father. The Bible is a love letter from our heavenly Father, and as we read it, it encourages, esteems, and affirms his wonderful love for us and the plans he wants to reveal as we walk with him.

"The thief (devil) comes only to steal and kill and destroy; I have come that they may have life, and have it to the full" (John 10:10 NIV). He wants to steal our joy, kill our peace, and destroy our hope! We must keep our eyes on Jesus and be in his Word daily to reveal the lies that we have been fed. He wants us to have the full, abundant life.

I really began finding the balance of this love relationship with Christ when my children started getting older. I realized that I didn't need them to *do* anything, just come hang out with me. They never said, "Okay, I will, Mom, as soon as I do all these household chores, mow the lawn, and do some of your errands, then we could sit down for fifteen minutes between the hours of 7:00 and 8:00 a.m. on Thursday." Guilty! That's just what I do to God.

One of my sweet memories is when my last child, as a senior, would come through the door after school and holler at me, "Hey, Mom, you wanna go to the woods and look for arrowheads and snakes?" You bet I did! I would go look for *mucus membranes* if it meant spending time with him! I never said no.

My kids also helped me find freedom and direction during my time of prayer with God. It became evidently clear that I could talk to God about anything I wanted my kids to talk to me about. For example, if I said, "Your birthday is coming up. Give me an idea of what kind of bike you want," and they answered, "You're so wise. Nevertheless, not my will but thine be done, my dear mother," I would be perplexed to say the least. I want to know what color, what brand, what size of tires. I love you. I want to do this for you. I want it to be a great gift!

If it's over the top, I might have to scale it down or explain why that mountain bike isn't what you need on these rural roads in Kansas, but I still want to hear what's on your heart. I would then expect him to trust me with the final decision. But come on, help me out here! Even if we already know what they want like God does with us, we still want them to ask and to see that we desire to bless them and to just spend time with them.

Another area where I have had to change my faulty thinking was in regards to confession and seeking forgiveness. After I had deliberately sinned, would God really be interested in hearing from me? Of course he would! I wouldn't want my own children to avoid me for a few days. No, I would want them to seek reconciliation as soon as possible.

I've also wondered if my confessed past sins might be holding up answers to current prayers. Can you imagine a father saying, "Son, I know you have your driver's license now and want to borrow the car, but I was just remembering the yellow spray paint you used on the back bumper when you were four years old, so hand me back those keys." Thank the Lord it doesn't work that way with our heavenly Father either.

What if my child was avoiding me and listed off reasons why he didn't feel worthy when questioned about it? "I didn't have a gift or flowers to bring you. I felt like I took too much of your time yesterday. I forgot to do some of my chores. I told my friends I was mad at you." Any of these responses would make me sad. None of these things matter to me. "You are my child!"

Father, am I really worthy to stand before you for anything? Do I deserve your attention? Have I earned it? Will I lose it

Carole Dougherty

tomorrow? Why in this huge universe would I ever think that you would care about me? "Because ... you are my child."

It has been three years since I took that study. I was glancing through the workbook recently and came across an exercise where we had to rate on a numbered line how confident we were that God loved us. I had circled an eight out of ten. A couple of years before that, I would have circled a five. What surprised me was that if I answered that question now, it would be an easy ten. I have been going through the hardest struggles of my life recently, and yet I feel loved more than ever. How does that happen?

I never grow weary of hearing the story of the Prodigal Son. I think it's because I relate to everyone in the story. I am the parent who has a wandering child and whose eyes are fixed on the horizon, watching intently for her to come home. I am the older brother who feels jealous and unappreciated when a younger sibling gets attention after misbehaving. I am the unworthy prodigal who doesn't understand this love my father is lavishing on me.

> But while he was still a long way off, his father saw him and was filled with compassion for him; he ran to his son, threw his arms around him and kissed him. The son said to him, "Father, I have sinned against heaven and against you. I am no longer worthy to be called your son." But the father said to his servants, "Quick! Bring the best robe and put it on him. Put a ring on his finger and sandals on his feet. Bring the fattened calf and kill it. Let's have a feast and celebrate! (Luke 15:20b–23 NIV)

I was beginning to learn that God is love and that he could *not* not love me. It's who he is. He doesn't change according to my good and bad deeds. In fact, he loves me so much that he died for me before I knew him. So now that I know him, why would my slipups, even deliberate ones, affect his love for me?

"You see, at just the right time, when we were still powerless, Christ died for the ungodly. Very rarely will anyone die for a righteous person, though for a good person someone might possibly die. But God demonstrates his own love for us in this: While we were still sinners, Christ died for us" (Romans 5:6–8 NIV).

How does he practically pass on this love? Well, for me it was answered prayer or a Bible verse that gave me hope when despair was settling in. It was my mom showing up at the front door because God laid me on her heart or God being my song in the night when I didn't think I could breath. It was his constant provision for me. All of these things shouted, "I love you. I am right here. I know!"

Journal—Oct. 5

Lord, I have a heaviness this morning. Emily, Gary, and I have work that needs done on our teeth. Christmas is coming, and we have no extra income this year. Gary is at the shop with a car that needs a new transmission. Our boat is still broken from this summer. Blaine has medical bills, and our savings account is dwindling. The engine went out of Emily's car, Lord. That's $1,400. Now they say I need a root canal. Help me to trust you. Forgive my unbelief.

A couple of weeks later I went to the mailbox, and there was a check from the government for $286. The next day there were two checks for $286. The following day there were two more. I called the agency to report the mistake, and they said that we had overpaid an adoption bill when one child was in state custody years ago. We were free to cash the checks. Over the next week, we would receive a total of $6,500!

Journal—Nov. 11

What a great Christmas! This money has helped with new phones, a Christmas vacation in Branson, a root canal, motorcycle parts, paying off medical bills, work on a transmission and a new engine in Emily's car! Lord, I want to please you with my life, my time, my bills. Thank you!

No matter how long I would have stayed up nights trying to come up with a solution to that huge dilemma, I wouldn't have come close to what he already had planned. Only God! He must love me. He does love me. His grace is unlimited.

The more difficult the trial, the faster you want to fall at his feet when he delivers you from it and the more you believe that you'll never doubt him again. We know that's not true, but each time we wonder if it's possible. I know that life is so much easier for me than it used to be because I can look back at his faithfulness and know that he will deliver me time after time. I don't struggle as often, and when I do, it tends to be short-lived.

"They will have no fear of bad news; their hearts are steadfast, trusting in the Lord" (Psalm 112:7 NIV).

"The Lord is compassionate and gracious, slow to anger, abounding in love" (Psalm 103:8 NIV).

"See, I have engraved you on the palms
of my hands" (Isaiah 49:16 NIV).

"Return to your rest, my soul, for the Lord has
been good to you" (Psalm 116:7 HCSB).

He dispels my fear, gives me peace and constantly reassures me of his love.

"Catch for us the little foxes" (Song of Solomon 2:15a NIV). Is there anything cuter than a baby fox? I would be tempted to let them get as close as possible before they damaged anything in my garden. That way I could enjoy the pleasure of them first before running them off.

Isn't sin just like that? Actually, it is right outside my door. How did it get that close? "If you do what is right, will you not be accepted? But if you do not do what is right, sin is crouching at your door; it desires to have you, but you must rule over it" (Genesis 4:7 NIV).

After this scripture was shared in church one Sunday morning, I asked Maisie to sketch out this visual for me. She drew a hunched-over, contorted demonic figure crouching down beside my bedroom door. I needed to be reminded of this threat, so I placed the sketch on my fridge.

My bedroom, a place for restful sleep and refreshment, would soon become the corner in my life where my most damaging battles would take place. Whether nightmares, unrealistic fears, or just the inability to sleep because of worries or concerns, the night was not my friend, and I would come to dread it. Waking in the morning would bring sadness, depression, and scrambling to find some hope to get me out of bed.

It wouldn't be one big sin that was chipping away at my relationship with God. It would be the *little* foxes that I was not ruling over. Actually, I didn't know that I could. I truly felt like I was a victim in chains and someone else was holding the keys. All I knew to do was to try to trudge forward and pray for release.

What if it's God that has the keys and it's him that is keeping me chained? What if I am feeling the *heavy hand of God* for a reason? After parting the Red Sea and the Jordan and swallowing up Pharaoh's army, Joshua says, "He did this so that all the peoples of the earth might know that the hand of the Lord is powerful and so that you might always fear the Lord your God" (Joshua 4:24 NIV). Should I be in fear?

Before my mother came to the Lord, she had been in a strict religion based on works and the fear of hell. She was terrified her children would go there as well, so she kept us constantly fearful and confessing our sins to stay on the straight and narrow. Even after I came to Christ, that guilt was hard to shake and became a way of life for me.

That faulty thinking made me turn everything inward, which caused me to feel that I must have done something wrong, and I was simply getting what I deserved. *Once again, I must not be pleasing you, and I must accept this as your will.*

Stormie Omartian shares, "Unfortunately, we are all susceptible to being deceived in some way. Deception is Satan's plan for our lives. But here's the good news; We don't have to listen to his lies. Yet we do have to examine our thoughts in the light of God's Word to see if they line up properly, because the devil will use everything you don't know about God against you." Is there a better reason to be in the Word?

Figuring out God's love, grace, and will for me each day is such a joy for me now. Letting him lead, take the reins, and even take me on detours gives me peace where at one time that lack of control only gave me anxiety. I want to stay so close that I can hear him whisper. And I don't really worry much of what other people think of me anymore. That is a pressure I don't miss.

Keeping me blindfolded and having to trust him every step of the way for many years would force me to hang on tight and listen very carefully for his voice. That bridge, that transition from the life I knew to the one I am living today was horribly difficult. The lies I believed about myself and God were so deep that nothing but the weariness of the journey would force me to get out of bed, grab my Bible, head outside, and be there at first sunlight to gather strength.

I would learn to pray, not to get things I wanted but to truly find out who God is and to remember that he is *for* us, not *against* us. I learned that he lets us get angry with him and question his ways, but he doesn't want us to stay there. David laments in the book of Psalms, "Why are you so far from saving me, so far from my cries of anguish? My God, I cry out by day, but you do not answer, by night, but I find no rest. Do not be far from me, for trouble is near and there is no one to help" (Psalm 22:1b–2, 11 NIV).

God would purge from me the need to schedule my own life but not to quit dreaming. He sometimes would drive the whole trip, and other times he would give me the freedom to set the course. Sometimes it was scenic and still other times dark, rough, and rocky. But I would learn that I could always trust him to lead.

The challenge that came out of St. Augustine's sermon on 1 John 4:4–12 was, "Love God and do whatever you please: for the soul trained in love to God will do nothing to offend the One who is Beloved." I love that! But he had to *train* me to learn to love him before I could experience that freedom, before my chains would fall off, and before I could stand up straight, free of the weights that kept me from running this race called life.

Chapter 5

A Shrinking Violet

I don't recall the first time or the last that I received a phone call from the school concerning Rebekah's headaches. I do remember the countless hours trying to figure out the source of her pain. "Did you drink chocolate milk at lunch?" "Did the janitor just clean your desk with a chemical?" "Did it happen after or before you came in from recess?" Nothing ever made sense. It was another typical trip to see the school nurse and then a quiet ride home with Bekah curled up in the back seat.

Rebekah was our *shrinking violet*, an extremely introverted, gentle soul raised right in the middle of her rowdy, free-spirited siblings. We often had to cut everyone's conversations off at dinner when we saw she had something to say and then invite her to share. When everyone stopped and stared at her, she would change her mind. Gary would see her as shy and fragile, but I saw her as very quiet yet strong.

Bekah would soon begin to miss family meals as she would often retreat to her dark, still bedroom. Mornings were always difficult to get her ready for school, and on weekends she would often return to bed shortly after rising. She had a permanent nest on the couch and often had to wear sunglasses indoors.

Eventually, she could not take glasses touching her head.

Rubber bands, hair clips, even hats and scarves were all avoided. She couldn't bend over without added pain, so Gary bought her a pickup wand so that she could clean her bedroom floor. I could no longer light scented candles or blast my praise and worship music. The list of foods that would make her even sicker grew continually.

We had to choose our vacations carefully as the altitude in the mountains as well as the sunshine on the beach caused too much pain. Car rides brought nausea, and campfires on camping trips were out of the question. Meanwhile, I am relentlessly researching day and night for the cause and effect. Well-intentioned friends and family members had endless suggestions that we usually checked out, but to no avail.

When she was in the seventh-grade, after several different doctor visits, a family practitioner offered to put her on some strong pain pills. Knowing nothing about the negative aspects of these drugs, we were thrilled. I remember thanking the doctor for finally giving us our daughter back. This physician simply figured it must be migraines, and we moved on ... for a little while.

I simply share with you the following because the higher we escalate, the steeper the descent.

Rebekah was literally a straight-A student from kindergarten through high school graduation. She was the kid who was asked to stay in from recess to help the one who had fallen behind. Bekah excelled in spelling and geography bees, speech competitions, and class elections. Out of thirty-some piano students, her teacher told me that she had two that she felt were gifted. Rebekah was one of them.

She would score in the top 2 percent in the country on national academic tests, and she was a natural at her ballet recitals. Now because of the medication, she would be allowed to pursue these interests a little more freely.

Bekah's passion was playing keyboard for the church worship band. She loved music, and she loved Jesus. And there couldn't be a better combination. One evening a Christian rock concert was held in the church gymnasium for teenagers. All of the band members were adults except a cute little seventh-grader on the electric guitar. Even though this boy and Bekah were friends on the worship team, she refused to stand, scream, and carry on with all the other *immature* girls when Addison walked out on stage. She would continue to play "hard to get" until they officially *fell in like* at the age of fourteen and fifteen.

Something else happened to Bekah that year. The headaches came one day and never left. She would not experience a day now without a headache, and they would grow worse, sending us back to the doctor and emergency room multiple times. We feared that she had become dependent on the pain pills and decided to fight the battle ourselves. That winter was grueling as we experienced our first journey of withdrawal, hoping to eliminate rebound headaches. It did not solve the problem.

We had pulled her out of school at the end of fifth grade, hoping to get a handle on her illness so she could return for high school. She was now a freshman, but she couldn't read without severe nausea. She had received her driver's license but could no longer drive.

After bringing her back home, I tried enrolling her in class up in Fort Leavenworth, where some of the officers were teaching economics to homeschoolers. She could not finish the course. We eventually quit dance and piano, recreational sports, and our church youth group. She was growing weaker, only able to eat fewer and fewer foods and sleeping her days away.

Addison was an old soul at a young age. He did not enjoy the nonsense of high school and was thrilled to find out that he could graduate in three years if homeschooled. Addison was playing eight different instruments by this time, and he hoped to pursue his dream of audio engineering and build sound equipment to his heart's desire.

I offered to homeschool him, and he joined our family. But basically, he was self-taught. A whiz at science and math, he was handy to have around the house the years I taught algebra and geometry. When Rebekah's condition worsened, Addison offered to read her assignments to her. This was a great help as he and Rebekah were taking advanced classes together. It also left me free to teach the others. We were homeschooling five that year.

⁂

My spiritual life waned during these years. It was just choked out with busyness and distractions. Determined to be the hero, I spent the little excess time I had trying to break the code of Bekah's mystery. I fell on my face, exhausted every other day, begging for answers and deliverance, never realizing that the process I was going through was much more valuable to God than just my suffering coming to an end.

I rarely had peace or joy during these years. I would see my other children and even my husband disconnect from Rebekah's suffering and pain and go on with their lives. I couldn't do that. I couldn't just say, "I am tired of all this. I think I'll just go shopping and buy myself a new pair of shoes," while she was lying on the couch, literally thrashing in pain.

I knew that trusting God was the answer. It's always the answer. But if you've ever had a long trip home with a toddler screaming in their car seat the whole time, then you know how the anxiety and frustration can throw you into a frenzy! Trusting God at that moment just doesn't seem to have anything to do with the answer.

Not only were Rebekah's activities becoming simplified, but mine were grinding to a crawl. I never felt I could leave her. The other kids were driving, so I wasn't needed to run everyone around anymore. I quit every committee I was on, ceased teaching Bible study small groups, and stopped volunteering as a youth coach.

Since I was home all the time, I began to grow gardens. It was so helpful with the healing because I finally had something responding to all my hard work. I became interested in herbs and found it fascinating that the Chinese had discovered ten thousand medicinal purposes for them. "And God said, Behold, I have given you every herb bearing seed, which is upon the face of all the earth, and every tree, in the which is the fruit of a tree yielding seed" (Genesis 1:29a KJV). So many mysteries to discover!

I began leaning toward the homeopathic side of health, teaching workshops on herbs, gardening, farming earthworms, making herbal teas, and composting. We would later begin raising our own chickens for eggs and bees for honey.

Rebekah and I began visiting naturopaths, but with disappointing results. She simply never responded to anything they ever had her try. Some were very mystical, leaning toward New Age reasoning but always sounding sensible. Wikipedia sheds some light on the subject by explaining that at the "Core factor of the New Age movement is its emphasis on healing and the use of alternative medicine. The general ethos within the movement is that health is the natural state for the human being and that illness is a disruption of that natural balance."

I agree with most of that definition, and some of the alternative practices, such as acupuncture, magnetism, and herbalism, have validity; however, other options such as altered states of consciousness, channeling, and crystals made me very uncomfortable. I know I still have so much to learn, but I now realize that things I once thought were dangerous have scientific and medicinal value. We simply commit to pray about everything. Sometimes our spirits sensed that this was not the place we needed to be, while other times we found that the same healing practices were found in God's Word.

The next few years were just shooting arrows without a target. God was very quiet during this time, and my days felt like I was riding a stationary bike as fast as I could. It would take the evening before I realized I hadn't gone anywhere. The next morning, I would climb back on, still worn from the previous trip and knowing I probably wouldn't be going anywhere again.

We had Bekah's orthodontist remove her braces early, hoping to remove strain. We were told she had slight TMJ, so we went to physical therapy to stretch her facial muscles in hopes of alleviating pain. An optometrist would clear her from any eye problems, and blood work for deficiencies came back normal. None of this was covered by insurance.

Chiropractors were not covered either, but so many people swore by them, so we kept revisiting those who had success stories. We spent a considerable amount of time at five different practices, paying extra for x-rays and experimenting with the latest gadgets and machines.

After a full examination, a chiropractor confidently said, "I know exactly what's wrong with her." He sarcastically went on, "This isn't rocket science. She has a blocked occipital nerve, and I can fix that." I started to cry. I told my husband later that I wasn't sure if I got emotional because he claimed to be able to easily fix her or if I was incensed at his arrogance and quick diagnosis. Either way, he was wrong, and she gained no relief.

We traveled four hours to the Mississippi River in Missouri to see a seventy-four-year-old chiropractor that had a remarkable reputation. The owner of the bed-and-breakfast where we stayed in this small town said she had many guests who had come from all over the world to be treated by him. He spent about twenty minutes with Rebekah and said he wanted to see her again in a week. He would do a more thorough diagnosis, and he was sure he could help her.

The next week after finding someone to be with the remaining kids at home, we set out for the river town again. Fifteen minutes before arriving at his office, we received a phone call from his receptionist saying that he had fallen and broken his leg. He not only couldn't see her but wasn't rescheduling. But she did add that there were other chiropractors in their town if I was interested. No, thank you. We were from a suburb of Kansas City where there were plenty of random doctors.

I remember the severe headache I had on the way home and the inability and the lack of will to talk to God during the whole trip back. I was more than weary. I was wondering if he was the God I had known him to be. Maybe the deists were right. You created the world, and then you stood back and let humans run it. You gave us brains, and you expect us to use them without consulting you. You really can't be bothered by the details when there are causes to be waged and wars to be won. "I can't do this anymore! I *won't* do this anymore!"

Two hours before hitting Kansas City, the traffic stopped. We were on a two-lane highway, so I took a random country road, trying to go around. I had no clue what I was doing. We crossed over the six-lane highway that we needed to be on to go back home, but looking down, I could see that all three lanes coming from the city were packed and at a standstill. And there were no cars at all on the road going into the city. Driving on, I ended up in a small town where I pulled into a random driveway. The family was in the yard, watching the unusual amount of traffic go by.

The man came to my window and asked me if I needed to get back to KC. He said I needed to listen very carefully and do exactly as I was told. "You will be going against traffic, and you will think you are wrong. But remember, listen to me and do exactly what I say." He gave me the typical country directions. "Go down here a ways until you see a giant oak tree near a cattle gate. Turn left and go until you see the white house with the broken shutter."

On and on he went while Bekah was trying to write it all down. One more time before he left, he said, "Do exactly what I say. Don't follow the crowd. Now ... what did I say?" I repeated it back to him one more time. Sure enough, as we left, dozens of cars were coming toward us, and no one was following us. We were on a beautiful country detour, passing cow-laced meadows and white farm homes with brick silos. I began to relax. I began to cry. God gave me grace, and I knew he was right there in the car beside me. We made it home with very little delay.

That night on the six o'clock news, I saw the chemical spill that had closed Highway 36. I also saw the thousands of cars that were totally blocked for three full hours. I knew I had not been following Jesus. I had run ahead of him and was wasting time, energy, and money. I was listening and following the crowd. "Listen to me and do exactly what I say, and I will get you through this maze with Rebekah." He was chipping away at my self-sufficiency one failure at a time. I apologized, and we became friends again.

Specialists seemed like the next option, but it was a new year with a new deductible. Our small town had secured the interest of a large casino to go in on the north side of town. This would include our ten acres, and I was sure this was God's way of providing our medical needs through this sale. We waited for more than a year for the news only to hear that they had changed their minds and were going a little farther north next to the Kansas Speedway.

When I heard about their decision, my heart sank. We had experienced several more disappointing doctor visits lately, and the casino had been our hope. I went outside and sat alone on our wagon wheel bench, and the anxiety began to rise. I began to cry, and then I had a rare panic attack where I couldn't breathe. It felt as if the top of my head was going to blow off. It frightened me, and all I could do was call out, "Help me, Lord. Help me!".

I began to calm down, and then I clearly heard in my spirit, "I am your hope, not the casino. I will take care of your needs. You are the one who assumed I would use the casino. I did not tell you that." I immediately was jerked back to reality, and my breathing slowed. A half hour later, right before we lost evening light, I walked back in to the house, ready for God to give me my new marching orders. Hope deferred again. But I was okay ... again.

The second neurologist that God directed us to was one of the biggest cheerleaders that we would have on this journey. He loved Bekah and Addison. He had a daughter their age who was in a worship band, and he just had so much empathy for her. He agreed to take her on at seventeen, even though he usually only treated adults.

After a myriad of tests, his diagnosis was just severe daily migraines. He felt the other symptoms that she had begun exemplifying were unrelated and needed other specialists. Over the next five years, she would go from one prescription to the next and would have to suffer through another withdrawal from pain pill dependence. He cared deeply for her and was almost as frustrated as we were at the lack of results. He somehow managed to give us hope each visit by assuring us that the answer was right around the corner.

During this time we were also regulars at a pain clinic. One trial drug or vitamin after another proved useless. She received occipital nerve shots and cold laser treatments, but nothing relieved her pain. They wanted her to return, but like so many other treatments, we just finally would have to move on.

At home we were experimenting with different research that we had come across, usually on the Web. We tried removing gluten, dairy, sugar, and acidic fruits. We eliminated anything fermented, vinegar, salad dressings, and everything pickled. We tried diets of juicing only, coffee enemas, and fasting. We were organic gardening and tried vegetarian only.

Storm fronts brought about totally dysfunctional days. But so did warm fronts, cold fronts, snowstorms, and tornadoes. When the tornadoes in Moore, Oklahoma, struck six hours south of us, Rebekah was bedridden all day. I would check the forecast for the barometric pressure regularly. We seemed to have our own family meteorologist.

Her senior year was tough, but with Addison at her side, they both graduated on time. He would start at the local junior college, and he hoped to be accepted into the electrical engineering program at Kansas University. For Rebekah, we had no idea, just the hope that help would come from somewhere soon.

Her neurologist strongly believed Bekah shouldn't go to college. He felt she wouldn't be able to keep up attendance, her grades would suffer, and she would eventually quit. That was so hard for us to hear. We had watched one passion after another be stripped from her. What of her future, Lord?

The fall after graduation, Bekah and Addison came to us with a plan. They wanted to get married. They could live in our basement apartment, and I would be there during the day with her while Add was in school. They had been dating for four years, were committed to staying pure, and wanted to marry the next summer. Having prayed together about it, they felt sure God was close to a cure and wanted our blessings.

Surely, since this was all falling into place, God must have something around the corner. We agreed but insisted on paying for anything medically that concerned her health. I can't imagine what all was going on in the mind of Addison's parents during this time. They loved Rebekah and just must have felt the same hope that the rest of us did. They gave their blessings as well. His mom, Amie, and I were great friends and the joy of working together for this celebration gave a new sense of expectation to both families. Saying yes broke all the rules, but we were all ready for some much-needed joy and laughter!

I want to stop here and share with you my *two steps back*. The afternoon I started writing this chapter, I felt a terrible and dark sadness. The oppression became so strong as I entered back into the memories of this season. I started to cry, so with a house full of family, I made my way to the bedroom, where I told the Lord that I didn't think I could finish this book.

It is haunting to revisit times of loneliness and fear, times when you felt God had abandoned you. I hated remembering that lie I had believed. As I lay there on the bed, I heard God say to quit writing about Rebekah now and write about him. "Remember my grace in the midst of all of it. Tell them about that."

When company left, I shared everything with my husband. When he prayed over me, the sorrow left, and I was able to find peaceful sleep that night. The next morning over coffee, I asked him where he thought all that panic and anxiety had come from. How was my faith different back then compared to now? At this stage of my life, I had so much joy and rarely suffered sadness.

A couple of hours later, a friend from my prayer team would text me with a simple message. "Love this, Carole. 'We are living for God and no longer living for the blessing'" (Oswald Chambers). I wrote her back to share last night's struggle and told her that this text nailed it.

I had been living for what God could do for me, dictating instead of praying, and I now wanted God's will more than anything. Earlier, I had not learned to wait on the Lord. Like a young child ringing the neighbor's doorbell and running away, I had dumped my requests at his feet and never stood still long enough to hear a reply.

In Genesis, God tells Abraham that he's going to have a son, and then after some time passes, Abraham questions this message. Then we see God's response. "As the sun was setting, Abram fell into a deep sleep, and a thick and dreadful darkness came over him" (Genesis 15:12 NIV). In the next chapter, Abraham had still not learned to wait on God but would jump ahead and have a son through Hagar.

"Abraham went through thirteen years of silence, but in those years, all self-sufficiency was destroyed" (Oswald Chambers). God motivates us through our pain to run to him. Distress just has that way about it. His Word says, "Do not let your hearts be troubled and do not be afraid" (John 14:27c NIV). But isn't fear sometimes the catalyst that drives us to want to know his boundless love? I just was tired of a troubled heart. And I so wanted peace back then, but I couldn't find it.

There is something about suffering for a long time that short bouts of pain cannot achieve. You simply get worn down. You begin to lose the confidence in yourself to problem solve. Your ability to shoot from the hip keeps failing. Your friends have run out of advice, the instructional manual is dog-eared and faded, and you get stuck on hold, paralyzed so that you can't move forward. It's humbling.

You are no longer the go-to person. You don't want anyone to ask you for advice. I found I could go to Walmart, the bank, and the library and never look anyone in the eye. Our family's motto was "We are here to serve, not to be served." I had nothing to give, and I didn't want to serve. I wanted to sleep. The Spanish priest St. John of the Cross would call this time in one's life "the dark night of the soul."

But there was grace. God gave me a strong marriage, and though Gary was working sixty hours a week so I could stay home, he strongly supported the many directions we took with Bekah. We would spend thousands of dollars on her, but God always provided. And we never went into debt. I had amazing girlfriends on my prayer team that I know had to get sick of my whining but never gave up on me. The basic structure of my life stayed intact though we were no closer to answers.

Chapter 6

Thorns and Roses

The Free Dictionary defines *maverick* as "a person who shows independence of thought and action by refusing to adhere to the policies of a group to which he or she belongs." This would be our oldest daughter, and the group she was refusing to adhere to was *the family*.

Emily was physically abused at a young age by someone she trusted. Floundering in the years that followed, I always wondered if we had done enough. There was counseling, therapy, and new protective measures taken, but we wondered how this was going to play out down the road.

In junior high she began to not want to play by the rules. She never talked back to me or ever said *no* to my face but would begin the deception and rebellion as soon as she walked away. She would let others take the rap for her without blinking an eye. Her lack of conscience when she got caught was stunning and greatly concerning.

My worst fear, though, was that she had no interest in spiritual things. She would willingly attend church and youth group but rarely internalized any of the teachings. She could lead in prayer, quote scripture, and sing in the worship band, but in her personal life, she was becoming very distant from all who loved her.

I wondered if Emily could even tell the truth as she seemed to need to embellish everything. I would ask her what time it was to test her. If it was 10:00, she might say 10:05. There was a compulsion to be in control, and she seemed to have no respect for authority figures.

Emily was such a *strong* girl, not just in temperament but physically as well. She joined the weight lifting team to help prepare her for all her sports and ended up winning nineteen gold medals in that field, some at the state level. Because of her can-do determination, she led her volleyball, softball, and swimming teams as captain of each her senior year.

If I needed help with a job, Emily was the best at assessing the work and the scope of the project. She had initiative and a high production level. She was such a hard worker, never having trouble finding employment.

Unfortunately, we began to get calls about her shoplifting. Emily was a very attractive girl, and it amazed us how she could talk her way out of being charged. One young policeman even slipped her his phone number, offering to counsel her "after hours." She was pulled over several times for speeding tickets, but she could usually sweet talk her way out of trouble, at least with male officers.

A probation officer called me one day from a jail in a neighboring town. "Go to the front desk, and pay your daughter's bail. And they will take you down to where they are holding her for shoplifting. You can pick her up there."

I asked the officer if she would see my daughter soon, and she said that she would. "Then will you please tell her that her dad and I love her too much to bail her out?" She said she understood and would pass on that message. We never knew how or when she got released that time.

Right after Emily graduated, we had a wonderful vacation. She was the usual life of the party, and it was good to have the family together. She loved to drive the boat, and she pulled everyone around on skis one afternoon. The night before we left, she fixed us all dinner and cleaned up the kitchen in the condo we had rented, knowing the whole time that she was running away from home as soon as we returned.

Emily was a thrill seeker, and we would lose her to a partying college town just thirty minutes away. She would spend many years addicted to drugs and alcohol and in and out of abusive relationships. The young adult that would later emerge was a mere shadow of the girl God had created her to be.

No one plans on having a prodigal child. You look back with sadness and wonder, *If only.* And you look forward with fear and ask, "What if?" It takes a wise parent who's strong in his or her faith to say, "So be it. What now, Lord?" Gary and I were not there.

We made a rule that we could not talk or pray about Emily at bedtime. It just too often would end in quarrels and sleepless nights. In the morning I was back to praying, "Protect her, protect her, protect her!" I was literally afraid of her dying from an overdose or drinking somebody under the table. I would get up at one or two o'clock in the morning to look at her Facebook page. I could see her steeped in a world that dragged so many deceived kids into its lie. It made me so angry that it was almost impossible to sleep.

I attended the conference of Christian author Beth Moore when she came to Kansas City one spring. I was convicted that I was filling my mind with visuals that could only do me harm, causing fear and despair. My mom reminded me that the father of the prodigal son did not read his son's diary every day. He just watched on the horizon for him to return.

I stood up at Beth's invitation and committed to roll over onto God any care that was robbing me of peace, hope, or joy. I would not follow Emily online anymore. Doing so was actually paralyzing me, and it made it harder to pray in faith.

God quickly showed me that my eyes were on my problems, not on him.

> The word of the LORD came to Elijah: "Go and present yourself to Ahab, and I will send rain on the land." Elijah climbed to the top of Mount Carmel, bent down to the ground and put his face between his knees. "Go and look toward the sea," he told his servant. And he went up and looked. "There is nothing there," he said. Seven times Elijah said, "Go back." The seventh time the servant reported, "A cloud as small as a man's hand is rising from the sea." So, Elijah said, "Go and tell Ahab, 'Hitch up your chariot and go down before the rain stops you.'" Meanwhile, the sky grew black with clouds, the wind rose, a heavy rain started falling. (1 Kings 18:1, 42–45 NIV)

I am convinced that Elijah kept his head down between his knees because the absence of clouds would have shaken his faith in what the Lord said was going to happen. I needed to keep my head down to stay off of her Facebook so that I could truly pray without fear to the God who loved her and wanted his child to come home too. I kept that commitment and became much stronger as I placed her in his lap daily.

The prodigal son in the Bible demanded his inheritance, and his father complied. Gary and I had little to offer Emily at this time other than the car she was driving that was still in our name. We decided we wanted to give it to her free and clear.

One principle in God's Word is giving to your enemy and going the extra mile. At a very young age, I had learned from my mom that your enemy could be anyone you are angry with or anyone who takes from you. It could be someone who cuts you off in traffic or butts in line at the grocery store. Maybe a close friend stole your boyfriend or got your job promotion. In any situation, your resentment diminishes as you give to that person. It puts you in control. The person is not on top for taking from you, but you rise to the top because you gave.

If we came home from school and complained about someone, my mom always had a solution. By that evening she would have us cross-stitching some design to attach to the top of a jar of jelly beans to place in our *enemy's* locker at school the following day. It was a life lesson for us to see how a simple gift could save a friendship.

At this point we had not seen Emily for two months, but we had heard she had left for Oklahoma. We didn't know how to get the car title to her. We laid the matter before the Lord that morning in prayer and asked him to work it out if he agreed with this plan. We told him we were flailing and not experienced at this and really needed his help.

That very afternoon I had some errands to run, and I took a side road that I rarely ever drove on. Coming directly toward me was our car with Emily driving. She quickly turned down the first road to her right and ended up on a dead end. I drove up behind her and parked. My heart was pounding. I couldn't believe God had answered so quickly. I now knew this was his will and that he was pleased with our decision to give her the car.

We both sat there for a few minutes, and then she slowly walked up to my window. We exchanged simple greetings, and I shared the plan her dad and I had for the car. She never said a word. I handed her the signed title and told her we would give her two weeks of insurance. Then we would be canceling our policy. The same applied for her cell phone. She remained stoic. I explained we would not be helping for college with the relationship the way it was. I told her we loved her and missed her before she returned to her car. Later Emily would end up totaling her car, and the insurance money, she admitted eventually, went toward partying.

Back in Lawrence, Emily became very transient, taking various jobs and moving around with different people. We would drive around looking for her to take her out for a meal. Sometimes we could track her down but not always. Oftentimes when we would see her, she would have new piercings and tattoos. She looked so gaunt, so unhealthy, and she became thinner and thinner. I would always have a stress headache returning home from those trips, even pulling over to the side of the highway to get sick after one especially difficult lunch.

The saddest memory I have of that awful season with her came on a cold, rainy afternoon. I brought my mom with me to help me find her. I missed her so much that I just needed to see and touch her that day. I went to the place she was working, and she agreed to sit in the car and talk with us. I saw the track marks on her arm as she climbed in the front seat. She quickly pulled her sleeve down, and we all sat quietly for a while. I simply knew I couldn't talk without crying.

My mom began reminding Emily about how loved she was and how valuable she was to God. She challenged her to not give up and reminded her of the hope of a different life. Emily never responded, so my mom went on trying to encourage her. Finally, my mom leaned over from the back seat and put her arm on Emily's. "God is right here in the car with us, Emily, and he knows you are hurting. If you could ask one thing of him, what would it be?"

Emily was quiet as she leaned her head against the fogged window and wiped away a tear. Finally, she answered, "I would ask God to help me to *want* not to *want*." She then got out of the car and walked through the pouring rain across the parking lot and out of sight.

Emily would not come home for Christmas that year. It broke my heart. "Love's a deep wound and what is a mother without a child and why can't I hold on to now forever and her here and me here and why does time snatch away a heart I don't think mine can beat without?" (Ann Voskamp, *One Thousand Gifts*).

Emily would give birth to our first grandchild in late summer of that year. Was it God giving a gift to his enemy? Would Connor be the gift that would save our daughter?

When we think of heaven, we imagine it to be the best experience we could possibly enjoy. Hell is associated with just the opposite. Life, on the other hand, is a mixture of thorns and roses. Both of these grow simultaneous in this life. Ann Voskamp calls it the "ugly/beautiful." In the midst of a life-altering crisis, a baby can be born. A parent receives a grave diagnosis right after witnessing a son's graduation. We lose a job six months after signing a contract on a house.

This described our situation, and yet life could not stop

because of Emily's absence. There were four more children coming up behind her, and the alarm would still go off at 6:00 a.m. tomorrow. Humbled and moving a little slower, we shuffled through our days and endured restless nights.

Our home was built in 1964, and it had two bedrooms and one bathroom when we purchased it. Gary would add three more bedrooms and a half bath within the confines of the same square footage. When the kids were young, it felt a little small, but now with teenagers, we were busting at the seams. Everyone was dating and had at least one best friend they would bring home regularly.

Climbing into to bed extra late one night, I told Gary that I felt like I was always planning a meal, preparing a meal, eating a meal, or cleaning one up, but I wasn't complaining! I really did love this life, and the kids knew they could bring anyone over anytime. We would just involve them in whatever work or project that we had going on.

This year's project was our first wedding, and it was a happy diversion from not only our ceaseless worries about Emily but Rebekah's health as well. Bekah knew every detail of how she wanted her big day to play out, and this mom was anxious to make it happen. Determined to not go into debt, Pinterest became our best friend.

Bekah had the creative ideas but rarely could help carry them out. With Emily gone, Addison's mom, Amie, joined me as the second wedding planner, and we had a blast together, painting birdcages found at garage sales, scoping out meadows for wildflowers, and finding bargains on wedding apparel. We recruited friends, letting them do what they did best—decorating, flower arranging, or baking pies.

We decided to put all those kids who were eating and

hanging out at our house to work. The wedding was outside, and they would help haul what seemed like half of my house out to the field for the celebration. Tractors would escort the guests to the site and bring the wedding party down the lane to begin the ceremony.

The Lord would hold off the rain, and everything would fall into place. Emily was asked to be a bridesmaid, and though we were never sure if she would show, we felt like God would get her there somehow and refused to worry about it.

The Lord and I were not doing so well. Six months out from the wedding, Bekah tried a new procedure suggested by her neurologist, and we were excited with the results. Botox was in the experimental stage for migraine sufferers, so very few insurance companies would cover it.

At $1,000 per treatment, the doctor knew it was out of the question, so he would gather up left over medicine from vials not fully used and allow patients who were not covered try it. It seemed to make such a difference, and each time she got a little better. This was it! It came just before the wedding, so the timing was perfect. We had fought the good fight, and now we were ready to enjoy the blessing!

But just like treatments before that seemed to offer relief, this one began to wane as well. Now with just three months until the wedding and still no answers, we would be handing our daughter over to an almost nineteen-year-old with no prospective hope of recovery in sight.

My guilt was unimaginable. It was too late to change course. *Lord, we asked you to lead in this. What is going on? What do we do?* This was not the way I had envisioned life playing out. This was not how I had dictated it in my prayers.

The outdoor wedding went forward in full sunshine. Hay wagons brought tan bridesmaids, wildflowers in hand, down a beaten path to be handed off to handsome groomsmen. My husband escorted my barefoot, radiant daughter down the aisle to join her groom waiting just under the sycamore tree, which overlooked a large creek. Rebekah mentioned her pain pills making her sleepy during the vows, but other than that, it satisfied all of her dreams. It was a day saturated in God's grace. Addison and Rebekah rode off in Uncle Frank's black coup, and all was well.

Emily showed up for the wedding and looked beautiful to me. There were some chaotic moments and a few tears, but it felt like old times, at least for a day. And I thank the Lord that she was part of it. She was gone as quick as she came, and we really never knew where she went. I was able to give her a really long hug, and she asked me to pray for her before she left.

A year of planning and praying was complete. I had let myself get overworked physically and became dehydrated. I left the reception with a splitting headache and threw up several times when I got home. I collapsed on the couch and slept there all night in my wedding clothes. I would soon realize that all was *not* well.

I received a call the very next morning from Rebekah. "Something's really wrong, Mom. Do you have any suggestions? I'm in so much pain." In the next few weeks, we would see a gynecologist, a urologist, and a urogynecologist. Rebekah was having problems because of the inability of her body to regenerate the linings of her uterus and bladder. She was diagnosed with interstitial cystitis (IC) and ordered a whole new route of treatments.

Researching this condition was disheartening to say the least. It was described as feeling as though you had a hundred shards of glass inside you. It was chronic, and support groups and sex therapy was the recommended treatment.

"Lord, I can't believe you would give her another chronic illness unrelated to her previous pain!" I went into total denial. I had been having problems concentrating or making decisions lately, and I could not handle this new side of her illness.

One month after the wedding, I went to meet my good friend Kelly for lunch. It was her birthday, yet she handed me a gift as soon as I sat down. It was Ann Voskamp's book titled *One Thousand Gifts*. She told me to read it slowly, or else I would surely miss something. She simply said the Lord had laid it on her heart, and she knew I would like it.

For the past several months, I had been losing weight, struggling with sleep, and I didn't want to get up in the morning. I just had lost my joy and decided to deem this month as "Joy in July" with the hope of finding it again. I had asked God to please help me get it back as living without it felt like no life at all.

I quit watching the news, sent all heavy questions from the children to Gary, stayed off of Facebook, and met with the Lord every morning at 6:30 on our deck. At my mother's suggestion, I saw a doctor, and for the first time ever, I was diagnosed with clinical depression and put on an antidepressant. I knew it was a combination of mental, physical, and spiritual strain, but I just needed support. God was helping me sort it all out, and I felt his freedom to choose this course.

A couple of weeks later, I received a call from my twenty-six-year-old son, Blaine, who was driving a semi-truck. He was calling from Minnesota, where he had pulled off of the

Carole Dougherty

road after he had had some trouble breathing. We encouraged him to head to the ER, and we lifted him up to the Lord while waiting for a call.

Valley fever was the diagnosis, a fungal infection in his lung caused from living in or driving through dry, arid regions. He had just come through Death Valley in California, and a knowledgeable intern in the ER had made the connection.

He would come home, heal for a month, and then head back out. Soon he would return with even more serious health issues. Now diagnosed with Crohn's disease and colitis, he would eventually suffer a ruptured intestine, requiring a colostomy. He would stay in the hospital for four months, recovering from the surgery and learning to walk again because of neuropathy.

I would go to the hospital every day, return home to wrap up schooling with our last two boys, help with Bekah while Addison was in school, and get dinner started. I was responding to the uncontrollable activity in my life by just taking one step at a time. But I was also learning to give up control, and I cried to God one day in the car. "I give up, Lord. Help me to surrender what I think I want to what you know I really need. I don't know how. I'm tired. Please help me."

———— ❧❦❧ ————

I had started reading *One Thousand Gifts* in the middle of July and began medication by the end of the same month. Looking back, I knew God had answered my prayer to begin to find *joy* that month through this odd combination. It is said that we love certain books because the author has the ability to take what we are already feeling and put it into words, often poetically, which speaks to us on an even deeper level.

Her book was a mirror for me in which my flaws became so clear, so evident. Sometimes we don't want our toes stepped on, but I was ready. What I had been doing wasn't working, and though it had taken years, I was ready for God to change me.

She reminded us that the original sin in the garden was discontentment and ungratefulness. Look at all God had blessed Adam and Eve with in that garden, yet Eve's eyes landed on the one thing she couldn't have. "I moan that God has ripped away what I wanted. No, what I needed. Though I can hardly whisper it. I live as though He stole what I consider rightly mine" (VosKamp, 2010).

I believed I had the right to have Rebekah healed. She was the bite from the tree I had to have for my happiness, and God said, "Turn around and look at everything else in your garden that I have blessed you with!" I couldn't see it. I wouldn't see it. I felt like the cause was just, and I was noble for pursuing it.

I knew I was supposed to say, "Not my will but yours be done." But I couldn't. Could I really lay my Isaac down and let God take her life for his greater purpose? Not really. Could I ask for my thorn in the flesh to be removed and then accept when he told me that his grace was sufficient? With closed ears, I was convinced that he never said that to me, so I was free to keep begging.

Ann Voskamp has the reader look at the other gifts around them but also challenges us to name them, to list one thousand of them. They are everywhere, and yet after the first two hundred, I was stumped. "Do we truly stumble so blind that we must be affronted with blinding magnificence for our blurry soul-sight to recognize grandeur? The very same surging magnificence that cascades over our every day here. Who has time or eyes to notice?" (Voskamp, 2010).

But as you do notice, you realize you were never alone. His presence is in front of you, behind you, and all around you every day and every night! After a year and a half of counting, I realized

I had written my own prescription for health on the pages of my praise journal. I felt for the first time in my life that God loved me unconditionally with nothing on my calendar.

I used to holler and carry on when I walked through a spider web. Now I apologize. Have you ever really taken the time to watch them weave their webs? It's magnificence all around. You simply can't wake up sorrowful when you have to count gifts every day. You are on the hunt as soon as you wake up.

Before you leave the room, there are morning shadows on the dresser, the steady breathing of the one you love beside you, and the smell of coffee. You can't be filled with anxiety and fear when you are aware that the perfect one who casts out fear is leading you by your right hand, has a day full of surprises in store for you, and will never leave you.

"Perfect love drives out fear"
(1 John 4:18b NIV).

"For I am the Lord your God who takes hold
of your right hand and says to you, 'Do not
fear', I will help you" (Isaiah 41:13 NIV).

I was learning to sit quietly before him. I was learning to follow. I was being trained to fully rely on his direction, and it was bringing me *joy*.

Chapter 7

Kiss Me over the Garden Gate

In the fall of that same year, our church launched a campaign to raise money to build a children's wing at the church. Our congregation was growing, and the staff had leaned on God every step of the way. They wanted this project to be bathed in prayer, and I was asked to head up the prayer campaign.

I was still not in good shape. I figured I'd bow out, but I offered to pray about it. After doing just that, it was clear to me that God wanted me to say yes, but I couldn't imagine why! This was no small project, and I did not feel up to the task. The physical and mental part seemed taxing, but mostly, I just did not feel qualified to be leading anything spiritually during this time. I didn't want to mess it up.

As always, when we follow God's leading, it's for our good because he has something greater in mind. Doing this actually gave me a peace because I suspected that it was part of my healing and it would help restore my relationship with him. We so often think that he is calling the spiritual elite to run ministries and lead people in their faith journeys, but the truth is that he is calling dirty, uneducated fisherman who are willing to obey and trust him to equip them for the task he has called them to.

To prepare, I began reading about the prayer warriors of the faith, different men and women I had always heard quoted but whose stories I didn't know. Some were biblical characters, and others were historical figures of the faith beyond the Bible. As I read, I just couldn't get enough. At first, it seemed that during their lives they had been living in a different dimension that seemed impossible to attain for the average person. But God says that is not so.

"Elijah was a human being, even as we are. He prayed earnestly that it would not rain, and it did not rain on the land for three and a half years" (James 5:17 NIV). I wanted to learn more. I was so hungry for it. Is that level of knowing God really for the average person? I was on a quest to find out.

Make time to pray. The great freight and passenger trains are never too busy to stop for fuel.
—M. E. Andross

Time alone with the Lord Jesus each day is the indispensable condition of growth and power.
—Andrew Murray

There is not in the world a kind of life more sweet and delightful than that of a continual conversation with God.
—Brother Lawrence

Don't pray when you feel like it. Have an appointment with the Lord and keep it.
—Corrie ten Boom

Prayer is not learned in a classroom but in the closet.
—E. M. Bounds

I would rather teach one man to pray than ten men to preach.
—Charles Spurgeon

The value of consistent prayer is not that He
will hear us, but that we will hear Him.
—William McGill

"Lord, these men and woman seem to know something I don't know. Lord, teach me to pray. Give me passion to discover the power of this discipline that I have taken so lightly. I want to know you the way they know you. I want to desire to run to my closet to spend time with you, but I'm not there yet. Let me see the vision they had so that I understand the urgency and have the joy they so evidently display."

God began answering my prayer, but it didn't come all at once. I learned that my prayers truly initiated change of action and that spending that time in my closet gave me an understanding of the heart of God. I just began to go deeper, spending a little more time with him each day and learning to listen. He was healing me from the inside out, and I was beginning to find the peace I had lost somewhere along my stubborn way.

I liked hearing some of the personal experiences from my friends as to how they set up their prayer closets. I tried one suggestion of lighting a candle to remind me that Jesus is the light of the world. I was really lost in prayer one day, kneeling and leaning near the candle. And yes, my bangs caught on fire, and I had just cut them! So now I had to cut them again. The burnt stench was so bad in the bathroom trash can that I finally had to take it outside so I didn't have to explain the smell to anyone.

As humbling as that was, I know it made God laugh. Prayer is not a formal time for professionals but for the brokenhearted to pour out their pain to Jesus, friend of sinners. It became easier the more I practiced, and after a while, I wasn't as aware of myself anymore. I quit questioning whether I was doing it right or wrong. It's just getting real with God and receiving the strength to walk back out and face the day.

The prayer campaign was a success. The church raised the funds needed for the intended children's wing, and I learned an enormous lesson in obedience. The Lord knew exactly what he was doing once again.

I love throwing parties, and most holidays were celebrated at our home. This year my youngest sister, Amy, knew the struggles I was having and invited us instead to join them for New Year's Eve at her farmhouse in western Kansas. She offered to treat us to a huge seafood feast, cook it, and clean it up too, and she wanted me to just come and rest. What a gift!

A few weeks before this offer, I had been studying the story of the angel of God wrestling with Jacob. I couldn't understand why Jacob suddenly quit wrestling and yet still hung on, refusing to let go until he received a blessing. What kind of blessing? Is this something I am supposed to be asking for?

"So Jacob was left alone, and a man wrestled with him till daybreak. When the man saw that he could not overpower him, he touched the socket of Jacob's hip so that his hip was wrenched as he wrestled with the man." Then the man said, 'Let me go, for it is daybreak.' But Jacob replied, 'I will not let you go unless you bless me'" (Genesis 32:24–26 NIV).

On the way to my sister's, we stopped for pizza with most of the kids. We filled a large round booth, but we still needed a couple of extra chairs. I brought up this question about Jacob's actions and asked if anyone had an idea of what the blessing was that he was demanding. I got a couple of quick guesses, and then they gave me the look implying, "Really, Mom? Can we just enjoy our pizza?" I got the subtle message and realized I would have to ponder this question alone.

The two-hour ride always relaxed me, replacing any stress with energy. When I was growing up, my father preferred that we not talk in the car and that we sit on our hands to avoid horseplay. After having children, the natural fooling around and jostling in the car would cause much anxiety for me. Gary helped me learn what was normal and acceptable, so now I could lay my head back and enjoy listening to the laughter.

Seeing the flint hills always meant we were getting close. We could smell the cattle ranch before we saw it, and it was always a competition to call it out first. It's the Kansas version of the game "who can see the mountains first?" when heading out for a Colorado vacation.

You know you are *really* in the country when your neighbors can't hear you shoot your gun. Target practice and riding the four-wheelers were what the kids looked forward to the most, but a cup of coffee and catching up with my younger sister was enough action for me on this particular trip.

Her husband was also named Gary, a retired drill sergeant from Fort Riley who lived the motto "Go big, or go home!" He cooked and grilled that way too, serving us up a mess of jumbo shrimp and buttered crab legs for our holiday dinner that night. Later we would all find ourselves spread throughout the living room, rubbing our bellies, moaning, and trying to stay awake for the midnight fireworks and gunshots. Breakfast would be served on time the next morning because there were still chores to do on the farm, holiday or not.

After lunch, my husband and I would sneak upstairs to steal a quick nap. I could hear his rhythmic breathing as soon as his head hit the pillow, but once again, I was asking God to explain Jacob's actions. With Gary's arm around my waist, I must have just fallen asleep when I jolted up and immediately began crying. Gary sat up, grabbing my shoulders. He wanted to know what was wrong. I held out my hand to him and just kept saying, "Wait. Wait. Just wait!"

I had clearly heard God speaking to me, and I wanted to make sure he was finished. As I drifted off to sleep, I had heard him whisper to my spirit, "Carole, I have been wrestling with you, and you would not let go." I waited. I wanted there to be more, but there wasn't. But I *knew* that he was telling me that it was *him* wrestling with me over my girls and that I was doing the right thing by not letting go and that the blessing was coming.

That experience had a profound effect on my faith journey forward. I felt God's presence in my life like never before. I knew that everything I was going through was being filtered through his hands, and he saw and knew how hard I was trying to hold on. Knowing the blessing was coming, no matter what he deemed it to be, gave me a renewed hope and the strength to just walk taller.

I went back to my Bible, and Jacob's story was so clear to me now. In the wrestling, Jacob was so stubborn that God had to turn up the heat. "When the man saw that he could not overpower him, he touched the socket of Jacob's hip so that his hip was wrenched as he wrestled with the man" (Genesis 32:25 NIV). That muscle is the sinew, the strongest one in the human body. He went for what would hurt him the most.

God knew what would hurt me the most, what would get my attention quicker than anything, my children. God wanted my surrender, and yet I was so stubborn that he also needed to turn up the heat to break me. But somewhere in the night, like Jacob, I went from wrestling to clinging and begging for God to take over and choose the blessing for me.

I went home and felt God's grace, so I began weaning myself off of my antidepressants. I joined the prayer team at church and rejoined small group Bible studies that I had backed off from. Satan had convinced me I was so overworked that I needed to say no to everything when the truth was that I was avoiding that which would fill me, not drain me.

> God knows how to save for you the time you
> sacredly keep for communion with Him.
> —A. T. Pierson

Rebekah was getting worse, and Emily was living on the streets; however, I entrusted them both to the Lord ... again. I was still counting gifts and refusing to peer into the future very far. I clung to the promises once again that "he is for us, not against us," that "I am not alone," that he "knows the way that I take," and that he was leading me by my right hand.

Bekah and Addison were going to a new and thriving church in Lawrence, Kansas, the same town Emily was in. Addison was helping lead worship, and even Bekah was playing keys on her functional days. Years earlier after Emily graduated from high school, Rebekah moved down to the basement to a larger bedroom. It was also the same year her headaches came and never went away. She would never have a day without a migraine from this time on.

Now that they were married, she and Addison lived in the basement apartment, and Rebekah was becoming less and less functional. She was experiencing sleep paralysis and nightmares in the night and even during daily naps. Not knowing all that

Emily had been involved in when she was down there, we felt we needed a special prayer covering for that room.

Gary and I had never met anyone from their church, and yet on a Tuesday evening, about fifteen people drove the twenty miles and showed up to our house to pray. They had all committed to fast that day for Bekah and even for our Emily, whom they had never met. They arrived at 6:00 p.m. and would not leave until 11:00 p.m. on a work night! We had a time of praise and worship. Several shared healing stories that God had graced them with, and they had a prayer walk all through our house, saving the basement bedroom for last.

With Bekah and Add sitting on the bed, they anointed the doorposts with oil, which just represented inviting the Holy Spirit into this place. They prayed for answers, for healing, for grace in the wait, and for God to be glorified. These were strangers to me, and yet they had sacrificed food and time for my girls. Who does that? The body of Christ! This was the church at its best. Thank you, Lord!

A couple of days later, someone called Bekah and shared that while they were praying for her, they started thinking about mold and wondered if she had ever considered that. Two more people would call before the week was up, also mentioning mold, not knowing anyone else had brought it up. I remember telling her that since we had just prayed and three separate people had come forth with the same information, we simply must consider that it was from the Lord.

Our basement had flooded many times, and we had seen some mold but had always cleaned it up. Or so we thought. In the process of looking, we found some, not a lot. There was some in the sheetrock around the bathroom, some under the carpet, and also some under the nightstand by Bekah's side of the bed.

Their pastor and his wife invited them to come to Lawrence and stay with them for two weeks to test out this theory. Another friend from church loaned them their extra bedroom for two more weeks. Bekah was steadily feeling better, and we were optimistic!

Soon after that, they were invited to move into another church member's third-floor apartment, but sadly, she began to spiral and was soon back to where she had started. We were devastated. What was that, Lord? We thought we heard you. This would begin a very long test of silence from God to show what was really in our hearts. "Do you really trust me, or is it only when you can see and touch and hear what I am doing?"

Now Addison was her sole caregiver, and he was in his third year of college. He had been accepted into the electrical engineering program at KU. Add and Bek had both become self-taught photographers, and that's how they were making their living at this time, working around Bekah's health.

They soon would start their own business, and though there was no time to promote their new venture, God would bring them all the contacts they needed through word of mouth. Editing was something Bekah could do at home, which made it a good fit, and she was gifted at it.

Add would keep her going, helping with the shooting, doing the scheduling, making the calls, building websites, and setting up interviews. He would prepare her food, carry her gear, back photos up, give her neck rubs, and pray with her during the shoots to keep her going. Their business grew, and they would eventually be fully booked a year out, mostly with weddings and engagement pictures. But Addison's school began to suffer.

Between shoots, Rebekah was spending most of her time in bed. Because mornings were so difficult, she was missing more and more time at church. After much counseling, Addison decided to withdraw from school rather than see his grades drop.

We had totally lost all contact with Emily. She had given up custody of her son, and she was somewhere on the streets of Lawrence. We needed a new plan. We quit asking God to protect her. Our new consistent prayer was, "God, spare her life, but do whatever it takes for her to walk with you!" We prayed that every day for six months before we got the call.

"Mom, I am in rehab. Will you and Dad come?" Emily had moved to Topeka with a new boyfriend that had found her at a party. She was planning on leaving for California when he talked her into staying and gave her a place to live. He was older, and he was trying to get clean. He wanted to help Emily do the same.

We hardly recognized Emily at this point. Mentally, she was not the same girl—anxious, irritable, unfocused, incoherent, and trembling. We truly thought that she had just been *eaten up* and that we would never see our child before drugs again.

Over the course of the next year, we would begin to see healing, though it would be a slow roller-coaster ride. She soon began to visit the church that had prayed for her that night. Pastor Jared went out to visit her and her boyfriend, Jeff, and shared Christ with them. Emily was beginning to hunger for the life she once knew, but this was a new way of thinking for Jeff.

But with one kind gesture after another thrown at them, love won the day. The church took them on and carried them back to Jesus. They plugged them in and passed them around, serving them, answering the tough questions, and patiently waiting when Jeff and Emily would disappear for a while. The following summer Emily would be baptized in the city lake. She would reunite with her son, Connor, and she would even see his dad begin to come to church and worship with them as well.

"And I will restore to you the years that the locust hath eaten" (Joel 2:25 KJV). "I am the Lord and I will redeem you with an outstretched arm" (Exodus 6:6 NIV).

No one could have imagined the redemptive power that God would use for them or the glorious plans he had for these two in the very near future. Emily and Jeff would begin getting clean just one month apart from each other. With God's grace, they would give up drugs, alcohol, and cigarettes on that day and never look back.

I say I don't like change, but then that would include job promotions, the beautiful seasons, and new grandbabies. What I don't like is for my plans to be changed without being consulted. With our last four kids, all being a year apart, changes were coming fast and furiously now. We would have three children get married in six months' time and five kids waving goodbye in the course of a year and half.

Maisie, my four-foot-ten niece who joined our family years ago, would end up marrying Thomas, the now six-foot-four neighbor boy we had the privilege of raising as well. He would head off to the US Marines, and she would join him after nursing school to work in a prison near the base. She assured my husband that he must not worry. She knew she was small, but they would be giving her two weeks of self-defense training. That did not faze his concern one bit, but he was reassured as he remembered her playful, sassy, "don't tell me what to do" attitude, so he consented.

Our youngest son, Reed, and his girlfriend, Madison, had also been high school sweethearts. In fact, they had been to school together in our small hometown since the first grade. At nineteen they tied the knot under the same beautiful oak tree that my husband and I had married under in the back pasture beyond the pond. Because they were both continuing their schooling, we let them move into the now vacant apartment in our basement.

Gary strongly *suggested* to all the kids that they wait five years to have children. Reed walked up to me four months after the wedding, pale and talking very fast, "Madi was getting sick on birth control, and we were in the process of researching other meds. And yes, she's pregnant!" I froze, dived face-first onto the bed, held my breath for about thirty seconds, stood up, straightened my shirt, and smiled. "All right then. Let's do this!" That late summer, now just one-year newlyweds, they delivered our grandson right on his due date. Jace would keep his grandpa young and spry and ease this mom's empty nest heartache.

Emily and Jeff were married in the spring, and they already had one-year-old Eva Grace. God blessed their obedience as they were trying to honor and live for him now. They would move about an hour away; however, our relationship kept growing, and I cherished the times of getting acquainted with my new adult daughter.

Getting ready for bed one night, I ranted at my husband, "They're all gone. They left too fast. What am I supposed to do now?" He never looked at me. He just shrugged and said he had no idea. I had been raising children for thirty years and didn't have time to transition to anything else. I knew God would eventually show me, but I didn't want any downtime during which I would have to grieve.

I don't think it's possible to throw yourself into being a mom and not mourn when they leave. It is a loss, a huge change. I had been anticipating it for a couple of years and asking God to clearly show me direction ahead of time. He said no.

I suspect that Satan sends his best before God does, and I found myself refusing a lot of things that came my way. I would find myself begging, "Oh, Lord, please don't make me do that for the rest of my life!" I had asked him to give me passion and peace about his plan, and I simply wasn't feeling it.

Three months later I would be approached to help direct a woman's mentoring program at our church based on Titus 2:3. Paul encourages the older women to teach the younger woman to love their husbands and their children. At first glance that doesn't seem like something you should have to teach, but our young women in this culture are in trouble. So many come from broken homes. They are transient, so family is not always around, and many just have no good biblical role models. I couldn't wait to get started!

I also went back to school to become a master gardener. I loved a program in Kansas City through Catholic Charities, which worked with refugees, helping them garden, sell their produce, and earn enough to buy the parcels of land they were farming. They needed volunteers to teach them financing and take them to the farmer's markets.

I also needed to be available to help Addison with Rebekah, run errands or sit with her on really tough days when he had other responsibilities. His mom and I would help clean the apartment or do laundry when he fell behind. We had just dismissed a team of doctors that had been working with her for a year and a half with no answers. We were now under no doctor's care.

I don't know how she kept going at times, but she continued to cling to hope. God would often remind her of one sweet thing he did for her in high school. When she was sixteen, there was a church that was having a revival for an entire year. Prayer rooms were open and praise and worship continued for twenty-four hours a day for the full year. On the last day, my friend, Kelly, her daughter, Hannah, and I took Bekah there so the congregation could pray over her.

What a wonderful night! There were so many generous strangers lifting Bekah up to the throne for healing and encouragement, for peace and the strength to trust. On the way home, we had to pull over for her to throw up. I helped her into bed, and then I fell into bed, disappointed and weary.

The next morning while I was having coffee, Bekah came and sat down beside me. "Mom, before I went to sleep last night, I asked God if he could just take away my headache for a little while because I couldn't remember what it was like to not have one. About midnight I woke up to go to the bathroom, and my head didn't hurt. I bent over to get my slippers, and it still didn't hurt. By the time I got to the bathroom, I started crying, and I just lifted up my hands and started praising God."

At this point I was feeling very sad because the headache was obviously back now. I couldn't imagine how disappointed she must be, and I put my arms around her. "No, Mom, I knew the headache would be back when I woke up. I just asked him to let me feel what it was like."

That experience gave her the hope that would carry her on for many years. She knew God was in control and could stop it anytime. She would tease and say, "I'm just a beach ball, Mom. Whatever he wants to do." I would often see her very worn and discouraged but never angry at God. She just wouldn't give up trusting in his plan for her life.

Chapter 8

Fruits of Our Labor

An *encourager* is simply someone who puts courage within. I tend to surround myself with these can-do friends because I am not as brave as I tend to put on. I hate that about myself. I can be on top of the mountain in the morning and then be blindsided by fear in the afternoon, curled up on the valley floor!

I wrongly think that my weekly, sometimes daily falls are of my own doing and that in order to be used by God, I have to pull myself back to the top. In reality, the strong, faithful Christians that he uses don't typically live on the mountaintop but are often in the valley.

The drab, mundane, boring valley—it's where he sees what we are made of so he can complete the work he started on the day that we met him. Those mountaintop experiences, camps, retreats, concerts, and conferences are all glimpses of God's glory to be put into practice in the valley of humiliation. It is not our sin keeping us here. It is actually God's will that we live here— except on special occasions when he wants to show us his glory to give us more fuel for the journey and recharge our batteries.

It's similar to our prayer life where we are asked to live by faith whether he grants our request or not. But every so often he lets us see magnificence through a crazy, unimaginable answer to prayer that just leaves you breathless and swearing you'll never doubt again. You wonder what you did different this time, yet you come up empty, trying to find a pattern.

Our family had all been in the valley for a while, and God seemed silent. We wavered, wondering if our crushing circumstances had gone unnoticed by him. Gary and I have one rental, an old farmhouse on seven acres near our home. We returned from out of town one weekend to find that our renter had taken off and the house had been trashed. Rent was due, and the rent we collected simply made our house payment. We needed a quick $2,000 to cover rent and all the damages and repairs, but we didn't have it.

Addison and Bekah were struggling financially with some school loans but mostly with a transmission that had just gone out. All of us had taken our needs to the Lord. We knew he would somehow provide, but we were still discouraged. We hadn't told anyone outside the family, so we were suspicious when two envelopes came in the mail.

They had no return address and the mailing address was typed. Opening them up, we found that each of us had received a cashier's check from an anonymous donor. The check for Gary and me was for $2,000, and Bek and Add's was $5,000! *This can't be real, can it?* We did all the detective work we knew to do, trying to decipher if this was legit and who would do this. We decided there was nothing else to do but head to the bank.

We went to the bank that issued the checks and explained to the two cashiers what had happened and why we were questioning them. We explained that we suspected it was someone from our church who knew the kids were having medical problems. The first cashier was cynical and huffed, saying she never heard of such a thing. The second cashier was a bubbly, young black girl who said church members had helped her out before and quipped, "That's just the way the Lord works!" She said, "I'll have to take them to the back and check with my supervisor."

She came back, waving them above her head. "They're real! You guys have been blessed!" The first cashier was actually stunned and went a little pale. I was hitting Addison's leg over and over under the table as they counted out the cash. When she was done, I handed a fifty-dollar bill to each of them, and leaving, I shouted, "Just payin' it forward. Thank you, Lord!" As Addison and I skipped out of the bank, I turned around to see the first one still looking stone cold while the other, obviously a believer, was singing and dancing in circles.

Gary had stayed home to be with Bekah, but they were both watching for us when we drove up. I think they could tell the verdict as soon as we sprung from the car. To have a burden like that lifted is beyond words. You just want to go find some rocks and build an altar or something. Saying, "Thank you, Lord!" just didn't seem sufficient. I love the mountaintop.

<hr>

Each year Christmas seemed to be the benchmark where we would compare Rebekah's progress with the Christmas before. She was now twenty-three, and she had been married for three and half years. The holiday would soon be upon us. She was definitely worse, and we were under no doctor's care. Because my mornings were a little freer now with everyone gone, Gary and I decided to meet at 6:30 a.m. to pray for Bekah every morning for the whole month of December. We figured we might as well add the other seven kids to the list.

In the past Gary and I had prayed together off and on but never as a routine. He would rise at five o'clock to do paperwork while I was usually getting breakfast, overseeing chores, and getting ready to sit down and teach school by 8:30. We were now ready for our little experiment and looked forward to getting started the following weekend.

Besides spending some time in God's Word, we would read the daily "Jesus Calling" passage by Sarah Young. We just found it made us more aware of his presence and his desire for us to take life a day at a time. Next, we would go deeper with Oswald Chambers in his devotional *My Utmost for His Highest*. We had to usually read that a couple of times to grasp the profound truths he would expound upon daily. After that, we simply divided the kids up, always ending with Bekah, asking for healing, encouragement, direction, and answers.

At the end of December, we had an amazing amount of answered prayers. Jobs were going well. Marriages were thriving. Everyone seemed extra blessed—except Rebekah. We still realized we needed to continue through the month of January so we committed to that as well. I grew to love and look forward to that time with Gary. There is just something about placing your loved ones on Jesus's lap first thing in the morning that allows you peace the rest of the day.

By the end of January, all of our kids were walking with the Lord. I can't remember that ever happening. My friend told me to take a quick picture. It might be short-lived, but I'll take it! Everyone was experiencing successes in different parts of their lives that they hadn't before—except Rebekah. We were so moved that we committed to continue our morning prayer time until one of us died. It was *that* transforming.

We would eventually divide the week up and pray for other specific people on certain days, such as family members, friends, and missionaries among others. I used to wonder how anyone could pray for an hour, but it was getting easier. We were learning to not only intercede but to count our blessings, confess our weaknesses, and express our desire to know him better. We would eventually quit dictating so much and just thank him for what he was going to do.

During this time we were reading new books about the disciplines and joys of prayer. Because of Bekah, I would sometimes wonder if I was really saying, "Lord, teach me to pray," or was I looking for a formula, a combination, a set of keys? I wanted some knowledge that would allow me to tap into God's power and have him give me what I wanted, what I needed to be happy.

It had been five months of keeping our morning appointment when things began to unravel. I was thinking spiritual warfare, but I couldn't camp on that thought long as I needed to start mopping up ... literally! The spring rains brought torrid floods, which made our driveway look more like the Grand Canyon. The water hauled all our gravel through the yard, forming a rocky beach for our pond. This had been going on for years because of faulty drainage on roads, and my frustration with our city officials once again stirred.

Our fully finished basement was ruined, and we spent a week tearing out carpet and sheetrock and moving one son, his wife, and their baby back in only to have it happen again a week later. Each time we did repairs, and we were sure that we had solved the problem—that is, until the next rain came.

My journal entry from May 17 says,

"The house flooded again, and I crumpled to the kitchen floor, feeling so much despair ... insurance declined claim."

There would be three floods that month alone.

Our youngest son had injured his back on the job two months earlier and still wasn't receiving workman's compensation or unemployment. He was quickly going through all the savings that he and his wife had set aside to buy a house and get out of our basement. The company said they had to let him go since his strength was now limited, so he should have been receiving benefits. Eventually, he was told by both agencies that he didn't qualify for funds because he had quit.

This was so disheartening to my very honest son. He had not quit. He had offered to do anything else they needed while his back healed. The supervisor had even driven him home, apologizing that they had to let him go. Our son told him that it was all right, God was in control, and he knew that he would find a way to provide for his family.

He had previously applied for the Pipe Fitter's Union and had been waiting for a response. One thousand applications a year were considered, and yet they would only choose three. He had such high hopes for this opportunity, but what would he tell them now?

My birthday was in May as well, and upon hearing this news, I retreated to my *closet* for a little one-on-one with God. I realize I get a little dramatic when I'm tired, a little cranky too, but he invites me to come "just as I am." My heart was packed full as I began to write.

"Dear Lord, this birthday is the hardest one ever. Our son's back injury has caused a crisis, and we do not know what to do. Bekah is getting worse, and Blaine's off of work again because of his health. I have a headache from trusting in you, from trying to recall verses and promises that pertain to all of this.

My energy is gone from 'casting down imaginations,' from reining my thoughts in, from refusing to not be afraid of bad news, from rejoicing when I feel like crying. I am trying to not doubt in the dark what you have taught me in the light. I am weak from holding up our kids' burdens with shaky arms and legs. I am tired from surrendering my plans as I fight to open clenched fists. I am shouting, 'Anything but our kids!' I am worn from laying another Isaac down.

Lord, help me to surrender this mess. I am anxious, stressed, and physically sick. I am not using your tools to get out of this pit. I can't remember what they are!

I am drowning. Help me. Help my unbelief. I have no peace or joy, and I don't remember how to get it. I feel too distracted to minister, and my sadness makes me tired.

I am not looking forward to vacation, and I feel guilty for feeling like this, for writing all of this. When will I learn? Why can't I just be grateful for all of your blessings? I want to be brave, steadfast, and strong. You say you are a 'very present help in trouble', so won't you please help me, Lord."

<hr>

The next month the Lord would respond by giving Gary and me a proactive step. In most of the books we had been reading, there was almost always a section on *fasting*, which I tended to scurry through. I had fasted on very few occasions. But it was really hard for me, and I felt like I was playing a game. Learning that all the great prayer warriors fasted made me take a second look.

"Fasting is the voluntary denial of a normal function for the sake of intense spiritual activity. It is a sign of our seriousness and intensity" (Richard Foster). Gary and I didn't really know what we were doing, but we trusted God to show us. Our family was desperate, and we were running out of options.

It was July before we had a full day to get away from town to spend a day fasting and praying. I have a wonderful friend, Julie, who has a beautiful antebellum farmhouse overlooking a valley near the Nebraska border. It would be perfect! She was going on a vacation the weekend we proposed and gave us free reign.

It turns out that there is no one way to fast. It goes from the extreme restrictions of no food for forty days to giving up one meal to spending the time when you were normally eating with the Lord instead.

> Some have exalted religious fasting beyond all scripture
> and reason; and others have utterly disregarded it.
> —John Wesley

The kind of fasting our Lord wants is not bringing attention to some cause while tying ourselves to trees. The fast he calls for is not about my health or the secret thought, *Well, at least I might lose some weight.* He wants our undivided attention and to know there is nothing in this day, not even my need for food, that will deter me from spending time with him so I can clearly hear anything he wants to say to me.

Gary and I needed to bat the details of this trip around and see how it was going to play out. Could we drink coffee? Gary retorted, "Too pleasurable". I asked about V-8 juice. "Too filling." How about Gatorade? "Maybe … if it's sugar-free." We were obviously novices at this!

We started out at about 7:00 a.m. heading north, planning to come home around 6:00 p.m., at which time we would stop the fast. We wanted to guard our conversations and our radio time so that our minds were on Christ and the mission he had laid on our hearts. We had brought some good reading material from home and some supplied to me by women from our church who knew about our day. Our good friends, Mike and Polly, had even agreed to fast at the same time.

Polly's husband, Mike, was a fit former US Marine and yet had been sick as long as Bekah had. Our journeys of hope and disappointment had paralleled each other, which allowed Polly and me to become prayer partners. We would celebrate new treatments together and pick each other up, sometimes kicking and screaming, after they had failed.

We arrived an hour and a half later and unloaded the car. My husband pointed out the familiar song of the mockingbird as we headed up the brick walk. Butterflies were swirling in the gardens and a wonderful breeze came up from the valley on this hot July morning. The surrounding fields were full of soybeans, and we smiled at the old tobacco barn that had obviously seen better days.

We picked a swing hanging in a nearby Ash tree and just started talking to the Lord. We reminded him that we didn't know what we were doing and asked if he would please help us, forgiving our inexperience. We told him that in our hearts we knew he hadn't forsaken us. But he had been so silent the last few months, and we really missed him. We thanked him for all of his provisions, but we were heartsick that Bekah and Mike were hurting so much. We felt alone in our suffering.

Have we done something to displease you? No. Are we reaping our past sins? No. Are we refusing to listen to you or surrender our will? Maybe. Could I accept it if God said that Rebekah would bring him more glory in this condition and that she would know true wholeness only in heaven? I had never allowed myself to ask that question. I knew God had told Paul that his grace was sufficient for his situation, but I just believed that I had never heard that response. I had to persevere with asking for her healing.

Gary and I spent time in passages from the Bible that we felt related to our cry for fairness.

> Ask and it will be given to you, seek and you will
> find; knock and the door will be opened to you.
> For everyone who asks receives; the one who

seeks finds; and to the one who knocks, the door will be opened.

Which of you, if your son asks for bread, will give him a stone? Or if he asks for fish, will give him a snake? If you then, though you are evil, know how to give good gifts to your children how much more will your Father in heaven give good gifts to those who ask him. (Matthew 7:7–11 NIV)

We were honest with him. "We have asked for bread and feel like you have given us a stone. You said you wouldn't do that, so help us to trust you even though we don't understand."

We had a glorious day walking the bean fields and singing, crying out to God and being assured that he had heard us, that he was not mad at us, and that he was happy that we were asking for help with our faith. Other than a caffeine headache, we survived the day and knew that we had obeyed what he had asked of us, and that felt good.

That night we rested peacefully and got up early for prayer together before church. It was a time of thanks for the joy, peace, and renewed strength we both felt from the previous day. Both of us were exhausted though, and I remember we took the Sabbath literally that day with a little rest and relaxation. Sunday night a big thunderstorm blew through, and at 5:00 a.m. the next morning, we heard low voices coming from downstairs.

An hour later Madi and Reed came up the basement steps, both very serious and Madi obviously pale. Reed asked if they could both talk to us. We all found a place to sit in the living room, and Reed began telling us that Madi had had a dream she needed to tell us about. My first thought was, *Is this about Rebekah?* My heart started racing.

I zoned out the first part of the dream as it was lengthy and detailed as she talked about where she was and how the angel first began talking to her. I began to catch up and really listen when she asked the angel why he hadn't saved her sister and mother. He told her that God had given them free will and that it wasn't love if it was forced. Madi replied, "Then can you heal Rebekah?"

I sat back hard against the couch, pleading with God in my spirit, "Don't do this to me. Don't do this to me. Please don't do this!"

Madi had written everything down as soon as she woke up and continued to read to us from her notes. "The angel stepped back like he was put off by the question. There was a voice that sounded like rolling thunder, but I couldn't understand it. I could tell the angel was listening, and when it stopped, he said, 'This is a prophecy of the Lord. Look for a parasite in her head, and douse her.' Then I saw her head being tipped back into garlic water, and a crash of thunder woke me up after that."

Madi said she had woken up four times because of the storm, but the dream continued where she left off each time. After the last clap of thunder that woke her up, the storm stopped. Madi said it was the most realistic and vivid dream she had ever had, and she knew without a doubt that she had been visited by an angel.

We all just sat in silence for a long time. Nothing like this had ever happened to us before. Because we were praying and because we knew we can't put God in a box, we believed that he had spoken to us in a supernatural way. But what now?

It was a work morning, and Gary and Reed were barely out the door before I started doing what I do best—research. How did she get a parasite? Can they exist in your head? What is the best course of action to eradicate it?

Madi and Reed made a trip twenty miles west the next day to the kid's hometown. They were anxious to tell Bekah and Addison about the dream. Both of them were stunned and excited at the same time as they were expecting God to do something soon.

I was on a quest, day and night, for the next few days and running as fast as I could … way ahead of the Lord, I might add. The reason that I know I was ahead of the Lord is that the familiar anxiety was there and peace was not. By Thursday I was a wreck, highly stressed, exhausted, and fearful, coming up empty and struggling to sleep. What were we to do with this prophecy? We couldn't ask for a referral to an infectious disease doctor because someone had had a dream.

I knew I was in sin and asked God to forgive me again for going it alone and not waiting for further orders. Gary prayed over me that night, and I slept well. The next morning I awoke with the alarm, and the first thought I had after opening my eyes was, *I did not tell you to research. I told you what to do.*

"What? What did you tell me to do? Oh … douse her head." I didn't know how that would help, but I knew it didn't matter what I thought. God said to do it. Sharing this with Gary, we both knew it was a matter of obedience.

In 2 Kings, Naaman went to Elisha to be healed of his leprosy. Elisha told him to dip himself seven times in the Jordan River in order to be healed. The Jordan River was dirty, and he thought it was beneath him to do such a silly thing, so he walked away. His servant talked him in to humbling himself and obeying the prophet. He did, and he was healed.

It had been four days now since we had heard from Bekah and Add, so I decided to call and let them know about how our week had been and our thoughts about dousing her. They quickly said that their week had been exactly the same—overwhelming research with no answers. They were very anxious for us to come over and take the next step, the only step God had given us.

Just like fasting, we were lacking specific details for dousing. I looked up how to make garlic water, and typical of the Web, there was no right way. So … we steeped ten large cloves, poured them into some jars, grabbed a big glass bowl, and headed out to see the kids.

It was a beautiful evening. We were all full of hope. There were lots of jokes and much laughter that night, which had been lacking for a long time in this household. We all went around and prayed and then listened to some powerful praise songs that challenged our trust even when it was dark.

Addison shared with us that he had recently found Bekah sitting on the floor of their office, sobbing. She felt like everyone had forgotten her. No one invited her anywhere anymore, and she just felt like giving up. Addison just held her, reminding her that the Holy Spirit hadn't forgotten her and that God knew she was hurting. He went on to tell us that they were expecting something big to happen because they had run out of options. Then Addison said, "So let's do this!"

We headed to the kitchen and gently leaned her head down to the bowl in the sink. We laughed and took a vote and chose to pour seven jars of garlic water over her head. We then wrapped her head in a towel and helped her to lie back down on the couch.

To be honest, Gary and I were looking for a miracle, an instantaneous healing because of our obedience. Instead we visited for a while, knew she was hurting, and needed to go to bed, so we just hugged them both and let ourselves out. It was a very quiet ride home.

Chapter 9

Spring of Life

I chose three of my closest friends to take to coffee the next week—each separately—to share our new direction. They were women I highly trusted who loved Jesus and would shoot straight with me if they saw any red flags. None of them did, and they all felt hopeful that this was truly the miracle it appeared to be. They each encouraged us to wait patiently for the next step. They all agreed to be on a team praying specifically for us to hear God's leading. Their excitement made me excited!

The following week I found myself digging through an old trunk full of books. I had taught a small group Bible study to another group of college kids, and we had gone through the book *Seven Keys to Hearing God's Voice* by Craig Von Buseck. There was a section on prophecy, which to be honest, I kind of skipped through.

Growing up, I did not come from a church that taught anything about prophecy. I knew it was mentioned in the New Testament, and I was now anxious to know the context. It was also mentioned in the books I was reading on prayer, and all of the authors confirmed that there were times when God still used it.

Agabus was one of the New Testament prophets who warned of a famine. Barnabas was considered a prophet and the one who introduced Paul to the apostles. Besides Jesus, John the Baptist was the most widely known prophet in the gospels, foretelling of the coming of Jesus.

I found the study and began to take notes. "Do not treat prophecies with contempt, but test them all" (1 Thessalonians 5:20–21a NIV). The author would go on to list several ways you could know if the prophecy, vision, or dream was from the Lord. And honestly, I didn't know which one this really was considered to be.

First, the person must be reputable and of a good character. They must be encouraged to write it all down and not interpret it themselves. If you are told to do something, then you must do it, but we must wait patiently and not do something we weren't told to do.

Madi was a very reputable young lady, and no one told her to write it down. She just did so the second she got out of bed. We had done the only thing God had told us to do with the garlic water, and now we were waiting.

I also learned that often a considerable amount of time will pass between the prophecy and its fulfillment. Abraham waited twenty-six years for his son, Isaac. The Israelites waited more than four hundred years to be delivered by Moses. Jesus was the Messiah promised centuries before he was born. The apostles were told that power was coming to them, but they must wait in the upper room for the Holy Spirit.

Weeks and then months passed without direction for Bekah. Nothing. God was very quiet, and I kept hearing from the enemy, the same thing Eve heard in the garden. "Did God really say …?" At first, I would question the whirlwind we had just been through, but then I would close my eyes and enter back into that weekend of fasting and praying. I knew God was there. He was in those bean fields, his Spirit speaking to our spirits, and we knew he was fighting for us. We were not alone.

Gary and I began falling on our knees several times a day, reaffirming our trust in him, telling him we were in this for the long haul and we would not be moved. We were tired of dictating our plans to God, and we just wanted him to hold on to us and to be patient with us.

We were worried about Bek and Add losing hope. Several times when we would ask the Lord to encourage them, he would send someone along in their town to be a cheerleader and keep them going. Their church was pulling for them and helped keep their eyes turned upward on the tough days.

And the days were getting tougher. She was becoming less and less functional, and I would often come out to be with her when Addison had to leave. Those were the hardest days to wait and not pursue some sort of new treatment. She was averaging eighteen hours a day in bed, and Addison often would need to carry her to the bathroom at night. I loudly asked the Lord one night while driving home, "Couldn't you just zap her and heal her, Lord? I know you can do it!"

Every time I would start to talk myself out of waiting, God would send a song, a message, or a scripture to back me off. On one particularly difficult morning, we heard Habakkuk 2:2, 3 (NLT) in a Sunday sermon. "Then the Lord said to me, 'Write my answer plainly on tablets, so that a runner can carry the correct message to others. This vision is for a future time. It describes the end, and it will be fulfilled. If it seems slow in coming, wait patiently, for it will surely take place. It will not be delayed.'"

Another time I was just plain tired of hanging on and asked the Lord to please encourage me, to remind me of why we were waiting so long. I was putting on my makeup, listening to a podcast by the Quaker theologian Richard Foster. He was sharing the story in Genesis where God told Abraham to build him an altar, take certain animals, cut some in half, and place them on it. But the next verse baffled him. "Then birds of prey came down on the carcasses, but Abram drove them away" (Genesis 15:11 NIV).

He said he struggled with that small verse for a week, not knowing its significance or meaning but sure that there was one. He finally asked a colleague if he had any thoughts. His friend explained that Abraham had to shoo the birds away because he was trusting in a living God and he was waiting for his next instructions.

The natural thing after being told to build an altar and put the sacrifices on would have been to light it. But God didn't say to light it, and he wanted to do exactly what he was told and nothing more. That meant running the birds away while he waited.

I can't tell you how timely that word was for me. I told God that when he was ready for the next step, we were listening and that until we had confirmation and peace from him to move, we would keep shooing birds.

Bekah was now twenty-four, and our Christmas benchmark, came and went with no change in her health. There was still more laughter in the house this season simply because of the hope we all shared. Even when she had to remain in bed during Christmas breakfast, we all just hoped this would be the last time she would miss the event and celebrated without her.

At the end of every January, we would have a family weekend away. Christmas was packed away on shelves, and the panic of spring fever was already upon us here in the Midwest, so we were ready to go. This year we were going back to the Henry Dooley Zoo in Omaha, Nebraska. There was enough to do inside all day that the coldest weather wouldn't deter us.

We found a beautiful bed-and-breakfast farmhouse just outside the city that could hold all of us. I was so excited that Bekah and Addison were going to join us. "Thank you, Lord!" Each family drove separately, and we had fun texting photos of smiling kids in car seats and husbands filling up on junk food and bouncing to some tune on the radio.

Besides both toddlers falling asleep in their strollers, the zoo was a hit. We were off to get a quick supper before heading to the B&B. Because of her many food restrictions, Rebekah rarely could join in when we ate at restaurants. We had all grown accustomed to that, and we knew Addison would thoughtfully pack a simple substitute for her.

A big wrap-around porch with antique gliders was a welcome sight at the evening rest site, even if it was January. The owners said not to worry about the mud on our shoes and reassured us that the home was kid-proof. What a relief to hear with this crowd, especially having the grandkids! We had a fun night playing cards and board games, and we stayed up way too late.

The next morning Bekah couldn't join us for breakfast. She would miss out on the day of shopping and antiquing, insisting we all go ahead while she lay in a darkened car. She shared with me in private that she was very discouraged because she knew what had triggered this severe migraine. She was down to only one power bar that didn't make her sick, and this was all she had to take with her on wedding shoots. She was sure that this bar had sidelined her.

Addison ended up just taking her home as usual, and we ended up cutting the trip short as well. Madi and I were determined to work together to come up with a power bar that she could take as a substitute. Tomorrow was Monday, and we could shop at a health food store, so we began researching on the trip home.

⁂

While on the Internet, Madi began randomly researching parasites and interstitial cystitis. She actually had something come up, but it was found in Brazil. Bekah had been to Brazil three years in a row for mission trips, and the first time coincided with the year her headaches came and never left.

Upon more research, we found a video of a testimonial where the patient talked about the parasite having a nest in his head, which gave him excruciating headaches. The parasites were found in unclean water and actually bore holes near pores to enter the body. Addison also found a map that showed that there was an influx of this parasite in the very area where Bekah had served. Forget the power bars. We were on to something!

I had a friend in Texas whose husband was a doctor, and I let her know our new discovery. She email me back the next day and said, "You won't believe this!" She said her husband knew in junior high that he wanted to be a doctor, and his seventh-grade term paper was about this very same rare parasite. Her husband felt we now had a good reason for that referral to an infectious disease doctor.

The first doctor in Lawrence turned us down. All of her symptoms seemed unrelated, nothing like an infectious disease, so he said no. We then got excited when a local team of doctors at one of the best hospitals in the country seemed interested in her. But after reviewing her referral, which was primarily about her daily migraines, they turned her down as well.

It was now March, and we had been pursuing help for two months with no more leads. My good friend, Kelly, stopped me at church one Sunday and said that her husband had a friend that was an infectious disease doctor. She also knew his wife through their kids shared activities, so she would see if they could help.

This doctor was out of town on business, so for three long weeks, we went back and forth through the wife, sending Bekah's story and explaining our present situation. He let his wife know that he would read the emails and see Bekah when he got back in town. Another week went by before he told his wife that Rebekah was too ill and that his suggestion would be to take her to the Mayo Clinic. Ahhh! I hated to call Bek and Addison with that news. We were all so hopeful that this was the one. I put it off until that night, which gave the Lord just enough time to line up another option for us.

Addison reassured me that it was going to be all right because he recently found out that his personal family doctor wanted to see Bekah. A woman who went to their church worked for this doctor as a nutritionist and had mentioned to the doctor all that Bek and Add had been going through. She immediately took an interest because she had suffered with cancer, Lyme disease, and fibromyalgia and knew what it was like to suffer from multiple chronic conditions. During the appointment she listened—I mean really listened—to their plight. That had been rare among the professionals we had previously seen, and this was so appreciated, especially since they had only just met her.

She explained that she knew an infectious disease doctor that she had used and thought she could get them an appointment with him. She also offered to immediately write up a referral. The next day she had a three-page referral explaining their whole journey, ready for Addison to stick in the mail.

I was so impressed with this woman that I just had to thank her for her kindness. Addison gave me the address of her office, and I was able to drop off a small bouquet to her receptionist. I left a card telling her about what she had done for this mama's heart. I slept well that night.

❦ ⦿ ❧

A week after sending the referral, Addison called to check on the status. He was informed that the doctor wasn't taking any new patients. Addison was firm and reminded the nurse that the doctor promised to fit her in if Bekah was bad enough. She let him know that even appointments for his own patients were two months out, but she would see what she could do. She called right back, asking if they could come in Monday to fill a cancelation that just came up. Thank you, Lord!

Monday came, and while they were at their appointment, I busied myself in the gardens, waiting for their call. It was now the end of April, and new life was springing up everywhere, so it was pretty easy to find things to do. Three hours later, they drove up, wanting to share firsthand all that they had been through. Bekah looked worn out, and Addison helped her to a bench in the shade near the chicken coop.

He began sharing that the doctor had spent his whole time with them listening to their journey from the beginning. He seemed especially interested in why Bekah and Addison had moved to Lawrence in the first place. The doctor did not think the parasite from Brazil was the cause of all of her symptoms. My heart sank.

He told the kids his story of how he became an expert in the field of mold toxicity, how he now worked with the Mayo Clinic and a lab in Texas that tested for four rare strains. Because of her exposure to the mold in her bedroom all of those years, he strongly believed that he knew her problem and that all of her symptoms were related. He was so sure she had mold poisoning that he insisted they pay the $500 fee and be tested.

115

First of all, we had no idea what this doctor specialized in. We were just looking for someone who would see her. We all talked about the shock that the Brazilian parasite was not the answer. Everything lined up so perfectly! This especially bothered my husband. Why did God allow us to believe that for the past three months? After batting it around, we all realized that God possibly used it to open up the door for this infectious disease doctor to see them.

Saprophytic mold lives off of dead and decaying organisms while parasitic mold lives and multiplies off of a living host. He referred to it as a parasite in her sinuses. It was living in a nice moist cave, which was a perfect home for it to breed. "Look for a parasite in her head." It wasn't the wiggly worm parasite that we had assumed we were looking for, but it was a parasite nonetheless!

A week and a half later, we got a call from Rebekah with the results. She had tested positive for poisonous gliotoxins at four times the level of severe. The lab had just recently began testing for this fourth mold on March 26, one month earlier. If she had taken the test before that, this doctor would have missed it.

None of the other doctors were specialists in this field, and the test wasn't even available to them. If they would have tested for the other parasites, she would have had a negative result and would be right back to square one. God got her to this doctor and this test within one month of it being available!

Our joy was slightly diminished when the doctor shared that it could reach a cellular level and be in her blood as well. He had just declared another patient with mold toxicity cured after two years of treatment. It was extremely difficult to eradicate, and treatments included steroids, antifungal supplements, and antibiotics. For two years? Her body was so weak. She also had to be on a strict no sugar diet as mold multiplied with sugar. At least we had a diagnosis!

Most people get over symptoms as soon as they are removed from the toxins, but some are allergic or hypersensitive. In those cases, the mold remains, begins growing, and resides in the patient. There is often a mutated gene that does not detect mold, so the body doesn't know there is anything to fight. This is why she became so much worse when she moved down to Emily's room. If she had been upstairs, she would just have periodic reactions.

We now feel like it was also the cause of Emily's asthma, which she is now free of, during her years down there and my many bouts with pneumonia. Bekah began to get better when she first moved to Lawrence, but possibly the mold was already residing inside her and had begun to grow. When she got worse, we felt we had misread what God was showing us through the prayer meeting at our home that night, but we hadn't.

We also realized that God really was telling us to wait on him since the dream! He was saving us detours that would have robbed us of both time and money. We were learning to trust in the silence and listen to his still, small voice. When there was nothing we could do, we were learning to give thanks and to choose joy.

The following morning after the call from Bek, I was wide awake at 4:00 a.m. thinking about the second part of the prophecy that included using garlic. I got right up and began looking up the correlation between garlic and mold toxicity. Page after page talked about garlic being the number-one natural way to destroy mold in your sinuses!

It turned out that my fear was correct. Rebekah's frail body was too weak to take the harsh medicines. Almost from the beginning, she was doubled over in pain. Gary and I went out to stay with her one evening, and we were literally afraid for her life. She could barely open the door for us. The house was pitch black, and she was as gray as death. When we later got home, we began researching the homeopathic route. She could not take this for two years! The mold might be gone, but her liver would be shot.

God had encouraged the *natural* way within each of our hearts, so by the time we all came together to discuss it, we were in agreement. For the first time, Bekah was taking the lead, researching other patients who had similar stories and sharing all that she was learning. There were more than 250 serious conditions that mold could cause in the human body, so every story was different.

God knew her specific needs, and if he could speak to us in a dream and lead us to the right doctor for the diagnosis, then we had to know he was still fighting for us. We wanted it to be easier. Were there still possible spiritual lessons to be learned? Hadn't we learned all of them by now? Apparently not. It was time to get back on our knees.

Never are we more of a target for an attack from the enemy than when we decide to get serious about prayer. But I have learned to pay less and less attention to the devil and keep my eyes on Christ, especially when I'm trying to navigate the obstacles that Satan uses to try to block me. God wants us to learn to be intentional and have fortitude, to be brave and single-minded when we go to prayer. Just step over the hurdles and do it!

It is now May, and we are ready for the rainy season. Gary had rebuilt our front porch and poured new concrete for the steps, hoping to avoid flooding this year. I had always loved storms. My father was a tornado spotter for the local civil defense department, and I always tried to go with him to chase storms. Now I panicked when severe weather was coming, especially at night. I could no more sleep than if I was waiting for a burglar to break into my house. I would lie there, anticipating the bang on the door, usually around two o'clock in the morning, followed by a panicked voice, "Dad, come quick. Water's coming in again!"

Our house would flood this May three times back to back to back, and the driveway would end up in the pond. Reed and Madison, baby in tow, would move upstairs for three weeks, and I would hang out in my bedroom, recovering from gallbladder surgery, unable to help with the enormous amount of work. At least I had time to pray!

The next month I got a call from Gary saying he had fallen off a ladder at work and he needed me to come get him. X-rays would show that he had severely broken his arm and wrist and would be benched for a while. We had plans to put a sump pump in our basement the following Saturday to see if that could hold off the rains that were forecasted. That is a huge job requiring a jackhammer, which would be impossible for Gary at this time. Right before he canceled the job, our son and a good friend insisted on doing it for him. And guess what? Our house has never flooded since!

I was asked during this time to share a testimony at our church about what we were going through with Bekah. While working on my notes one evening, my son Reed asked why I was sharing when she wasn't healed yet. I had to stop and think about that. The truth was that I wanted them to know where we were now and not wait to present it until it was a nice, neatly wrapped package with a bow on it. This was where we were. This was what we were still waiting on. I was hoping people could relate to our story on some level.

I was right. My sister posted the video on Facebook, and people viewed it more than a thousand times in the first two weeks. There were more than twenty shares as well. Gary and I began receiving phone calls, texts, and emails from hurting people. Very few even mentioned Rebekah or Addison, but they needed to talk about their own crisis situations—divorce, prodigals, infertility, and other issues. They wanted to learn to trust, to learn how to really pray. They longed to know how to still be happy while they were waiting. Did God really love them? Had they done something wrong to deserve this?

I had no intention of ever writing a book. I didn't want to enter back into the pain or to have to relive it in order for the reader to fully understand. I was not up for that exhaustive work. But in seeing how relatable some of our experiences seemed to be, I told the Lord that I was open but that he would have to make it very clear. In the meantime, he sent us *more* opportunities to learn to trust.

While at the doctor for a routine check on his arm, Gary mentioned that he was short of breath coming up from the pond. The doctor suggested he might as well get that checked out now since he was on workman's comp. While he was being tested at the hospital, I received a call saying that Gary had what they called the "widow maker." He would not be coming home because he might not even make it through the weekend. The main intersection of arteries was completely blocked, meaning that death was eminent without surgery. She went on to explain that they were scheduling him to undergo a quadruple bypass open-heart surgery on Monday. Now that was definitely not on my calendar! I'd rather have had another flood.

The young surgeon took my number and insisted the kids and I stay home for the six-hour surgery and that he would call us when it was over. We made enchiladas together, and I let the grandkids keep me distracted. I lay down in my room for a while and listened to praise and worship to keep my focus on the Lord. I then realized that if this was the *widow maker*, I would have three days to plan a funeral. I began writing down the songs that I thought would glorify the part that God had played in Gary's life. I had such peace.

I think we all wonder what will come out of us when we are really squeezed. Is this life of Christ only true on sunny days? Is his presence really for the here and now?

I jumped when the phone rang. The doctor was happy to tell me that the surgery was a success and reported that Gary was doing well. I went right in and tore up that list. But I know, that if we are walking with God, our faith doesn't have to be diminished when a crisis strikes. His grace can cause it to be magnified.

When Gary woke up, they asked him what his pain level was, and he said it was a *six*. They asked him where it hurt, and he pointed to his wrist. Before the heart surgery, we had asked for a second opinion on Gary's arm because he was in so much pain. The physical therapist wouldn't work with him anymore because something was wrong and she was afraid of doing more damage.

While he was still recovering in the hospital from his heart operation, the nurse of the surgeon that had repaired his arm called me. She said that there was a problem and that they needed to perform the surgery again and take the hardware out. I kidded her and suggested they might have to get in line. After she heard the situation, surgery was pushed out to a later date to allow him to recover for a while.

Gary would be off of work for more than seven months, which turned out to be a perfect time for me to write about what

God was guiding our family through. God made it very clear to us through prayer that I was to do this and reminded us through his Word that although I didn't feel qualified, I could trust him to lead because he equips us for what he's called us to do.

Chapter 10

Lord of the Harvest

When I was a young woman in my twenties, I spent a day at home alone, fasting and praying for a baby. When a year had gone by and a child never came, I just figured it didn't work, or I had done something wrong because I didn't get what I had asked for. For years, I would never consider doing a day of fasting again.

But look at the size of my family now. God did hear me. "In the time of my favor I will answer you" (Isaiah 49:8 NIV). I was looking at that day all wrong. It should have been a heart-to-heart with God, baring my soul and placing my request on the lap of Jesus. It should have given me confidence that I had entrusted my desires to God and could leave the timing to him.

If I would have listened, he would have told me to go have fun, that he had me covered and that I need not be anxious. That's what prayer does for me now! If there is nothing I can do about it, then I give thanks, choose joy, and "do the task that is nearest at hand."

<hr>

Through the waiting, God has sprinkled our lives with blessings, true to his character. Our youngest son was found by a judge to have been wronged by his former company. Justice was served, and he was rewarded with lost wages, able to replace the savings they had lived on. He is now a proud member of the Pipe Fitter's Union and in his third year of school.

Blaine is healed up after several health scares, and he's back out on the road trucking. Maisie and Thomas are expecting a baby and heading home to Kansas to live after finishing his fifth year with the US Marines. Bobby and Billy are also living close now, so all the chickens are coming home to roost.

Oh, there's one more chick.

Our girl Emily has become the real deal! Next month, in November, she will have been drug-, alcohol-, and cigarette-free for two years. She is working with addicts in the local prison of her hometown and serving in prison church. She is teaching at addiction centers on Saturday nights and serving in her own church through the outreach ministry. Last Christmas she collected personal hygiene and toiletries to pass out freely to the girls coming in for help at the rehab center. They typically go without until they can raise money to purchase these items, which often takes weeks.

Emily told me once that she couldn't get clean in the house and neighborhood she was living in because there were too many triggers all around her. She said she couldn't even go back to the previous town she lived in because her old friends were everywhere and it would be impossible to succeed.

Oh, the Lord is wise! You guessed it. He made her stay right there in that house with those neighbors and in that town to show her that "humanly speaking, it is impossible. But with God everything is possible" (Matthew 19:26 NLT). She mentioned later that she would be running the rest of her life if God hadn't taught her that lesson.

A couple of months ago, the Lord blessed her and Jeff with a beautiful little house right in the middle of a wonderful neighborhood. God has helped her husband get more work than he alone can handle through a new remodeling business he has started, even hiring several more employees as the work continues to multiply. We will soon be joining Emily and Jeff as they celebrate Eva's third birthday. It will be the first party they have hosted since getting clean. I have always loved my daughter, but I really *like* her now and love hanging out with her and learning everything fresh through her eyes. Hope deferred? In his time.

⚜

"They will be called 'oaks of righteousness', a planting of the Lord for the display of his splendor" (Isaiah 61:3b NIV). I am claiming this verse for my kids! The problem is that my idea of bringing God glory through my kids is often bringing myself glory as well. Who knew all those times that I felt sick when Emily came in with another tattoo or piercing that it would open up doors and a ministry for her in the prisons? They immediately know that she was where they are now and that she *gets it*. All I could think of was that it would keep her from getting a respectable job that we could be proud of in the future.

> "It is good for me that I was afflicted,
> that I might learn your statues."
> (Psalm 119:71 ESV)

> "Before I was afflicted, I went astray,
> but now I obey your word."
> (Psalm 119:67 NIV)

If it's good for me to be afflicted, then it's good for them. Through prayer, we really can trust God to pinpoint the series of struggles in their lives that they will need in order to grow in

125

their faith. I needed to quit seeing these times as attacks from Satan with everything springing out of control.

It is a ridiculous notion that God would say, "Oh no, what am I going to do now? This dilemma has caught me completely off guard! Does anyone have a suggestion?" It reminds me to focus on his sovereignty in all situations. I must stop trying to alleviate the pressure that God puts on my family members so that he can do his work in them.

When I was a preteen, I thought I was a shoe-in for seventh-grade cheerleading the following year. That fall a new girl transferred to our school and won the coveted position. I was devastated, especially since my two best friends were also picked. To this day, I empathize so much with losers and run to their side to remind them of the hope of another chance. If our kids are always winners, where is the empathy? Where is the ministry?

As much as I want to protect and attend to every detail in the garden, there are elements I simply can't control. Even the proudest master gardener must acknowledge that. Having adopted children helps me understand more this notion that I can't be totally responsible for the way things turn out. I will love them and do the best I can; however, I don't fully know the hand that I've been dealt, and I have to really lean in hard for his help.

But the truth is that I'm not fully responsible for my biological children to turn out well either, not to mention my marriage or my job! It's all loaned to us for safekeeping to place back at Jesus's feet. And it was through his sovereign love that each one of these blessings was given to us, no matter which path he chose to bring these to us.

Gary and I love to take road trips. We especially love running into God's *remnant*, his believers, in remote towns like

Lesterville, Missouri, or Ash Flat, Arkansas. It doesn't take long before you realize he's teaching us all the same thing. I met Sharon, a mother of four in Lawrence, Kansas. She turned out to be a pretty wise mom, and we became Facebook friends. I caught some of that wisdom as she posted one October morning. She added that this principle gave her so much more freedom to relax and enjoy her girls.

> That's it, no more parenting out of fear! I will no longer pray for God to protect my children from every hidden danger in the world but rather that He will equip us, walk with us and turn any hardships they face into teachable moments so they are allowed to exercise their own faith while we are still alongside to help them walk it out. My prayer is for their faith to be their own, not mine, before they fly out on their own. So, give them the room to try their wings!
>
> —Sharon Struve

"Oh, Lord, help me to quit doubting your goodness when it comes to my family. You tell us in the 77th Psalm that you were angry with Israel because they didn't trust you with their deliverance. You also promise that, 'No good thing will (you) withhold from them that walk uprightly' (Psalm 84:11b NAS). Help me to focus on my own walk, and leave the care of your other children to you."

There are no such things as problems, just opportunities. Really? Because that is not my knee-jerk response to looming catastrophes! But I would like it to be. That's simply an example of *trust*.

> This is the trust I lack: to know that if disaster
> strikes, He carries me even there.
> —Ann Voskamp

I love that quotation! That's what I want, and it comes from gazing upon his faithfulness time after time after time! I need to quit imagining future disasters for my kids without also envisioning his presence and his grace that will get them through it. I need to even picture them standing a little taller because they are wiser and stronger for having gone through it!

In the last decade, team-building exercises have popped up in the workplace with the object of instilling trust and unity among employees. We used to do this in our youth groups as well, trying to bring the group together as teammates into the body of Christ. I loved the relay race where they were blindfolded and had to carefully listen to their partners, the designated callers, who were trying to help them make it around obstacles and get to the finish line.

If they listened intently to their callers' voices, they could maneuver the roadblocks and make it to their goal without even stubbing their toes. But the callers were allowed to disguise their voices and yell out to the competitors in the race, hoping to get them off track. You had to go slow and listen for the right voice if you were to succeed.

Nothing is sadder than looking back over your life and realizing that you did some major damage because you were listening to the wrong voice. You see the people you hurt and the regrets you can't take back, and you long for a do-over. Thank God this is where the cross comes in. With the cross, we get a do-over. Because Christ took our punishment, we are forgiven, and he helps us work out the consequences of our past failures through his grace. We must listen though to his voice going forward to experience this healing.

I find that I need to be very intentional about blocking out wrong voices in my life. If I have too much television, Facebook, or nightly news, I begin to wander. My spirit drops, and I don't even realize it. In finding the balance again, I gain freedom and peace when I choose to protect the voice of truth.

Most of the time, I hear the Lord's voice through his written Word, but sometimes when I sit silently before him in prayer, his spirit speaks to my spirit. I found myself lost in prayer after a very tough day right before Rebekah's diagnosis. After Gary left for an errand, I was able to be alone with God.

I am a visual person, and when I get on my knees, I picture myself before the throne of God. The Father is always just a silhouette of light in my mind, and I probably picture that because that's the way he's portrayed in those Bible tracts from the '70s. In her small group study on Esther, Beth Moore taught us that the kings could accept or reject you when you came before them. If they rejected you, your head was cut off, which made for a short visit. But if the king lowered his scepter toward you, then you were to place your hand on the circular end, and he would grant you your request.

This day I was desperate. I fell before the throne and visualized God lowering his staff, and I grabbed onto it. I pictured him asking, "What can I do for you?"

This day I had only one thing to ask. "Is there anything you want to tell me about my daughter Rebekah?" I was listening so hard and for so long, yet I heard nothing.

The Bible says that Jesus is at the right hand of the Father, ever interceding for us. I looked at Jesus and said, "Do you have anything to say to me about my daughter?"

I could imagine him smiling at me. I sat there for a full five minutes, staring at him, yet he said nothing.

Then my vision stopped, and God began to respond. I felt God lift the scepter as if to excuse me, and I fought with him, saying that I didn't want to leave, that it was safe in here, and that I was sad out there. Then I heard in my spirit Jesus say, "I will go with you." And I saw him walk toward me, take me by the right hand, and we walked together out of the throne room.

That day changed my life! I understood for the first time what *Immanuel* really stood for. That name given to Jesus meant, *God is with us!* We don't leave the throne room and come out alone. We don't leave God in church and then return to our lives. I knew this truth intellectually but not really in my spirit. I began feeling his presence in a whole new way.

Now when I go to my knees, I don't picture God on the throne and Jesus at his side. I see Jesus walking in with me, and then as I kneel, he takes his place at the father's side to intercede for me. When I leave, he walks out with me. I am not claiming anything doctrinal about this exercise for anyone else, but this visual helps me grasp the truth of Jesus being my companion day in and day out.

Sometimes he's still silent, but he's silently sitting in the car next to me. That's different than silent and distant.

> "Am I a God at hand, declares the Lord,
> and not a God far away?"
> (Jeremiah 23:23 ESV)

"Have I not commanded you? Be strong and courageous.
Do not be frightened, and do not be dismayed, for
the Lord your God is with you wherever you go."
(Joshua 1:9 ESV)

I don't have to be sad *out there* anymore because he's *out there* with me.

Sometimes we can get lost in prayer, and other times we only have time for a quick "Help me, Lord!" before we plunge ahead. I was sitting on the warm ground in my garden leaning back on my arms, catching a breeze when my phone rang. It was Bekah, my normally composed child, crying so hard I could not understand her. "Mom, everyone is celebrating like I'm already cured, and I still can't hardly get out of bed!"

She had encouraged Addison to leave and go play guitar with some friends. Somedays she needed him gone so she could just cry it out. She was good about that. Always aware and worried of his relentless caregiving, she would put on a tough front most of the time to keep him from stressing out. Their marriage was rock solid, and I never took that blessing for granted.

"Mom, I can't answer one more text saying, 'So how are you feeling today?' I just don't want to go anywhere or see anybody!" She knew family and friends meant well, and she felt guilty letting them down, which led to the pressure and panic she was feeling. I decided to get the word out for everyone to go through Addison or me when checking up on her, explaining her concern about disappointing them. Two years of healing was a long time to play the "nothing new" game.

On cloudy days when hikers can't see the summit, they inevitably slow their stride. When the clouds and mist give way to sunshine and snowcapped mountain becomes visible, everyone quickens their pace. We hadn't heard of anyone who had a story that was just like Bekah's, so we truly didn't know the path to the summit let alone what it would look like.

Bekah had found some similar stories online with patients who could not go the medical route. These individuals found some success through detoxing and healing the body (phase one) so that the body could eradicate the mold itself (phase two). But it's difficult to heal your body when the mold is destroying it.

Recently, we have found a kinesiologist who specializes in finding the body's priority healing needs. She is experienced in the area of mold toxicity and has agreed to be our guide on this journey. Addison's father, Jeff, who's also an amazing cook, prepares bone broth for Rebekah to drink every day. She is using strong probiotics and antifungal essential oils, such as lavender and frankincense, in her daily routine as well. Her diet is extreme. She doesn't eat any sugar. And she has happily lost fifteen pounds in recent months.

She is logging how much time she is in bed and how far she can push herself to walk daily. She is choosing to send one text or e-mail a day to encourage someone else. Bekah is trying to spend more time in the Word and watching her pastor's online podcasts until she can return to church.

She knows she will be back to playing keys on the worship band, so she works with Addison to stay current on praise music. As a couple, they have had multiple opportunities to share their faith and their story with clients who don't know the Lord and even counsel young couples who are having marriage issues.

Addison, the kindest and most humble young man I know, is a remarkable example of unconditional love and servanthood. Everyone's lives are touched just by being around him and seeing his contagious smile and his "can do" attitude. All of Bekah's brothers have high admiration for him, and they would tell you that he is their first choice as a role model.

The continual miracle through all of this is that they have kept every photography session they have been contracted out for. God knows this is their source of income, and he has faithfully gotten her through wedding after wedding. She might throw up on the way home or spend the next several days in a dark room, but he *gets her to the church on time.*

They don't just get through a wedding, they nail it! Bekah and Add have been featured in some of the most popular wedding magazines, and they are in great demand and booked up for months, sometimes years in advance. They know it's the Lord. They have no time or energy to promote or advertise their business. It's all word of mouth. They know it is grace and are continually amazed.

I began writing about our family's story while Gary was home recovering from heart surgery. Although we were still not seeing any progress with Bekah's pain, God clearly led me to start this book, not knowing how the last chapter would end. I wish this last chapter was different.

I still cannot present to you a fully wrapped package complete with a bow. We are still experiencing the *process.* "Hope deferred maketh the heart sick." But not anymore. We know where our hope lies. We know that God has heard us and that he is for us, not against us.

He knows the pain of our childhood, the sadness of divorce. He knows the loss of a child and the fear of losing our jobs. He sees each sleepless night and every shattered dream that we have ever had. Even when we didn't know him, he knew us.

He doesn't just know these things. He orchestrated them to drive us to himself so that "when he has tested me, I will come forth as gold" (Job 23:10 NIV). Everything we go through is about learning to trust ... everything!

What are we supposed to do in the wait? "Lord, may we not fear not knowing." He tells us that it is possible to be content while not seeing where we are going. The reason we can is because he knows and he is still leading. "Your path led through the sea, your way through the mighty waters, though your footprints were not seen" (Psalm 77:19 NIV). We really can live with our dreams and desires, just not concrete expectations. "It is not for you to know the times and dates" (Acts 1:7 NIV).

How can circumstances that sent me into a dark time of depression still exist but not have power over me anymore? Nothing has changed, but everything has changed. I am different. By choosing to strengthen my spirit every day in the hope that Christ gives me, I am empowered.

I do not wake up afraid that fear will overshadow my day. His promises give me a firm foundation to stand on, and claiming them simply drives out the fear I use to think I had to live with. The more time I spend in his Word, the more loved I feel, and it all seems to go together somehow.

> "No fear exists where his love is. Rather perfect love
> gets rid of fear, because fear involves punishment. The
> person who lives in fear doesn't have perfect love."
> (1 John 4:18 GWT)

God showed me his love at my Kerith Ravine, the place where he "whittled me down" as he did with Elijah. He took away my calendar and my ability to care for my needs, and he became my caregiver. When I was helpless, he became my companion. Through stripping away all my security, he showed me I was still *something* when I felt like *nothing*.

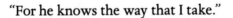

If in my lifetime I never get to enjoy a full day of shopping and going out for a *normal* lunch with Bekah, I have accepted that. I am literally more heavenly minded these days and I know we will have that mother-daughter date in eternity someday. I do believe God has us on the healing path right now, but I finally feel I have laid my Isaac down in Jesus's lap and picked her up for the last time … by God's grace … I hope.

But until the Lord takes me home, I am determined to count my gifts, stand on that mountain, throw my hands out, and fall back into his loving arms as many times as it takes until I can enjoy the ride.

"For he knows the way that I take."

Epilogue

Two months after turning my manuscript into the editors, I received a text from Addison. He simply said he needed to meet with me for coffee. My last conversation with him was discouraging. We had been to more than forty doctors and the latest one, the kinesiologist, wasn't working out. In all his research, he had found no doctors in the state of Kansas that could help with Bekah's diagnosis. He had located one in Chicago for an $850 consultation fee. This doctor was not covered by their insurance and did not Skype, so all appointments would mean traveling to the Windy City.

I knew Addison needed encouragement from me, but I didn't have any to give. Christmas was coming, and Bekah had gone downhill, so we were all struggling. I had always been able to encourage Addison before, so I knew I needed God's help. Anything I could think of to say just seemed rehearsed or repetitive.

Gary decided to fast and pray with me the following morning before meeting him that evening. By the time I left, God had laid so many things on my mind that I wasn't sure one visit would be enough. That is just like the Lord when we call on him—a very present help in times of trouble.

We met at a McDonald's on the highway halfway between our towns. There was a separate, almost soundproof room in the back that was perfect because there were a lot of tears that evening. In fact, I had never seen Addison in this shape before. Rebekah was now living in a dark room, and he shared with me that he had mentally planned her funeral that week and felt total despair.

I shared the scripture God had clearly laid on my heart. The book of James asks us,

> Is anyone among you sick? Let them call the elders of the church to pray over them and anoint them with oil in the name of the Lord. And the prayer offered in faith will make the sick person well; the Lord will raise them up. If they have sinned, they will be forgiven. Therefore, confess your sins to each other and pray for each other that you may be healed. The prayer of a righteous person is powerful and effective. (James 5:14–16 NIV)

We agreed that though we had done this five years ago, we needed to do it again. We left each other that night with the weight on our shoulders a little lighter, knowing God had directed us and given us a plan of action. Addison would contact Pastor Jared and ask for a meeting.

The Monday before that Christmas, Addison and Rebekah, a few family members, and several of their closest friends met on a bitter cold night at the home of an elder. Addison began by standing and nervously thanking everyone for coming. After a few second pause, he said he had something to share.

"You guys are my best friends. You have been asking me for months how things were going with me, and I have looked you right in the eye and told you I was doing just fine. Well, I have been lying. I am not fine. Actually, I am hopeless and depressed.

My wife is in bed every day all day, and that is why we are here." With that, he sat down and dropped his head in his hands.

A long silence was broken by the strum of Pastor Jared's guitar as he began a slow worship song. For two hours prayers were offered up between praise melodies and testimonies. The evening ended at 11:00 p.m. with people laying their hands on them for one final prayer. Gary and I were tired, worn, and disappointed that God hadn't blessed our obedience with a healing ... again.

⁎ᶜᵒⁱᵒ⁎

The next morning, I received an advertisement on my Facebook page from a pain clinic offering a free consultation. This office was less than ten miles away, so I began filling out Bekah's information out of habit. I almost immediately deleted it and then chided myself for being so gullible. I had done this so many times, running ahead of the Lord and costing our family time and money.

That evening I received an email from the same clinic asking if I was ready to sign up for my free visit yet. I stared at it, a little confused, and then deleted this message as well. The next morning I received a phone call from them. I explained to them that I wasn't sure how they got my info but that my daughter had been told that she had a rare form of mold poisoning and I was sure they couldn't help us.

The woman paused before replying and then quietly spoke, "Don't be so sure. I've had mold toxicity and found help." That got my attention. We began sharing our stories, and I found out she was from Rebekah and Addison's hometown, had lived on the same street as their downtown church, and was a Christian musician and songwriter as well. In fact, she said this pain clinic was Christian-based, and she shared some scripture that God had personally used to get her through her healing.

I shared with her about the prayer meeting we had just had and eventually about the dream that led us to the diagnosis in the first place. She was so excited and wanted to share Rebekah's condition with her doctor. She told me if he could not help her, he would be honest and say so. Well now, that was a switch from the many previous doctor's we had seen.

She was going to call me back within a couple of hours to share what she had found out. I wanted her to know that even if he couldn't help us, God had used her to encourage me and to let me know that he can pull an answer out from under the woodwork when he's ready. She prayed with me, and I could tell she was really pulling for us.

An hour later she returned the call only to say that her doctor felt that he could not help her but that he had a partner he thought could. I gathered the information, thanked her for everything she had done for me that morning, and told her I would let her know. I then called Bekah and Addison and shared the whole ordeal. We all felt that this could be God answering our Monday evening prayers and that we should at least check it out. Addison took the info, called the doctor's office, and took an available appointment, two weeks out.

Gary and I decided to meet Bek and Add at the doctor's office that afternoon for their scheduled appointment. It was a cold, dark, oppressive day, and I knew Bekah would be in extra bad shape before I even saw her. I was right. We had to move the scheduled meeting into a darkened room where there was a bed for her to lay down.

From the beginning, we were impressed with this young doctor. He was friendly, excited, and full of hope. He had all of her records spread about over his desk like a giant jigsaw puzzle.

He was familiar with her past doctors as well as the danger of her present condition.

After a three-hour consultation, none of us could see any red flags, and we all agreed to go ahead with the gamut of tests he insisted were necessary. They were very expensive, and because he was a functional doctor, they were not covered by insurance. We once again had to trust the hand of God that seemed to be clearly leading us to this juncture.

———————————— ✤ ————————————

It was a full month before Bekah and Add would get a text asking them to make an appointment to discuss the test results. On the following Friday, they went by themselves to an afternoon meeting. Gary and I chose to hang back and stay at home to pray, but after three hours, I began the familiar panic inside. What if he said they had found nothing and Bekah was too disappointed to even call? Then what?

I figured I'd get my daily mile in just walking the floors of my house and praying. I found myself crying to God out loud and walking faster the louder I got. "I know you told me to send Addison to the elders. I know we were obeying you by having that prayer meeting. Who else but you could make that contact pop up on my Facebook and then my email and then have them call me?! I know you had Jen call to encourage me. You gave us all peace when we went to see this doctor, Lord! If that wasn't you, then I don't know when we could ever hear you!" And then within minutes I received this text.

> Too worn out to give the full run down of the appointment, but to sum it up, my test results showed a lot of abnormalities and revealed a lot of reasons why I would be a chronically sick person.

So we have lots to work on in my gut, immune
system, hormones, neurotransmitters, adrenals,
etc. All which are suffering pretty severely right
now and need some help. He feels positive we
can do it. I'm just being a beach ball ☺. Will show
you everything on Sunday.

She would share later that he told her she had the body of
a very old woman, not a twenty-five-year-old girl. He said her
body did not even register any vitamin D, and her levels of the
fungal infection candida were off the charts. Is it crazy that this
was good news to me? After all these years, something actually
in writing! She said, "Mom, it feels good to see on paper what I
am feeling every day."

Addison even said that he was encouraged because the doctor
made it sound so hopeful. He had already set them up with a plan
to begin detoxing and rebuilding all the damaged areas. It will
take time to heal so many different areas, but he assured them
that this was what he did.

Only the Lord could have orchestrated this encounter with
this doctor. Although haunting and mysterious to us, this was
never out of God's reach or his power to reveal it to us. Why did
he wait so long? Why do we still have to wait for the final healing
to take place?

In the story of Lazarus, Mary sent word to Jesus in another
town that her brother was sick. The Bible says that though he
loved Martha, Mary, and Lazarus, he chose to stay where he was
for two more days. He reassured them that it was for God's glory
so that God's Son would be glorified through his act. Though our
hope is deferred, he has a plan. It's all about trust.

Could part of his plan be the book in your hands? Is he possibly going to comfort you as he has comforted us over and over, year after year? We are compelled to tell our story, to shout that he's real, that he lives within us, and that he is involved in every detail of our lives! He is faithful, and it's worth sharing our lives to tell others of what he has done for us!

Love so amazing, so divine …
Demands my soul, my life, my all!
—*Isaac Watts, 1707*

My Child,

You may not know me, but I know everything about you. Psalm 139:1 I know when you sit down and when you rise up. Psalm 139:2 I am familiar with all your ways. Psalm 139:3 Even the very hairs on your head are numbered. Matthew 10:29-31 For you were made in my image. Genesis 1:27 In me you live and move and have your being. Acts 17:28 For you are my offspring. Acts 17:28 I knew you even before you were conceived. Jeremiah 1:4-5 I chose you when I planned creation. Ephesians 1:11-12 You were not a mistake, for all your days are written in my book. Psalm 139:15-16 I determined the exact time of your birth and where you would live. Acts 17:26 You are fearfully and wonderfully made. Psalm 139:14 I knit you together in your mother's womb. Psalm 139:13 And brought you forth on the day you were born. Psalm 71:6 I have been misrepresented by those who don't know me. John 8:41-44 I am not distant and angry, but am the complete expression of love. 1 John 4:16 And it is my desire to lavish my love on you. 1 John 3:1 Simply because you are my child and I am your Father. 1 John 3:1 I offer you more than your earthly father ever could. Matthew 7:11 For I am the perfect father. Matthew 5:48 Every good gift that you receive comes from my hand. James 1:17 For I am your provider and I meet all your needs. Matthew 6:31-33 My plan for your future has always been filled with hope. Jeremiah 29:11 Because I love you with an everlasting love. Jeremiah 31:3 My thoughts toward you are countless as the sand on the seashore. Psalm 139:17-18 And I rejoice over you with singing. Zephaniah 3:17 I will never stop doing good to you. Jeremiah 32:40 For you are my treasured possession. Exodus 19:5 I desire to establish you with all my heart and all my soul. Jeremiah 32:41 And I want to show you great and marvelous things. Jeremiah 33:3 If you seek me with all your heart, you will find me. Deuteronomy 4:29 Delight in me and I will give you the desires of your heart. Psalm 37:4 For it is I who gave you those desires. Philippians 2:13 I am able to do more for you than you could possibly imagine. Ephesians 3:20 For I am your greatest encourager. 2 Thessalonians 2:16-17 I am also the Father who comforts you in all your troubles. 2 Corinthians 1:3-4 When you are brokenhearted, I am close to you. Psalm 34:18 As a shepherd carries a lamb, I have carried you close to my heart. Isaiah 40:11 One day I will wipe away every tear from your eyes. Revelation 21:3-4 And I'll take away all the pain you have suffered on this earth. Revelation 21:3-4 I am your Father, and I love you even as I love my son, Jesus. John 17:23 For in Jesus, my love for you is revealed. John 17:26 He is the exact representation of my being. Hebrews 1:3 He came to demonstrate that I am for you, not against you. Romans 8:31 And to tell you that I am not counting your sins. 2 Corinthians 5:18-19 Jesus died so that you and I could be reconciled. 2 Corinthians 5:18-19 His death was the ultimate expression of my love for you. 1 John 4:10 I gave up everything I loved that I might gain your love. Romans 8:31-32 If you receive the gift of my son Jesus, you receive me. 1 John 2:23 And nothing will ever separate you from my love again. Romans 8:38-39 Come home and I'll throw the biggest party heaven has ever seen. Luke 15:7 I have always been Father, and will always be Father. Ephesians 3:14-15 My question is…Will you be my child? John 1:12-13 I am waiting for you. Luke 15:11-32

Love, Your Dad,
Almighty God